100

· GREAT BREADS ·

PAUL HOLLYWOOD

100

· GREAT BREADS ·

Photographs by Neil Barclay

CASSELL
ILLUSTRATED

An Hachette UK company
www.hachette.co.uk

First published in Great Britain in 2004 by
Cassell Illustrated, an imprint of
Octopus Publishing Group Ltd,
Carmelite House
50 Victoria Embankment, London EC4Y 0DZ
www.octopusbooks.co.uk
www.octopusbooksusa.com

This edition Published in 2015

Distributed in the US by
Hachette Book Group
1290 Avenue of the Americas
4th and 5th Floors
New York, NY 10104

Distributed in Canada by
Canadian Manda Group
664 Annette St.
Toronto, Ontario, Canada M6S 2C8

US ISBN 978-1-78840-214-9
UK ISBN 978-1-84403-838-1

Printed and bound in China

For the original edition

Editors: Victoria Alers-Hankey
and Barbara Dixon
Photographer: Neil Barclay
Stylist: Fanny Ward
Design: DW Design
Jacket Design: Jo Knowles

For the new edition

Senior Commissioning Editor: Eleanor Maxfield
Art Director: Jonathan Christie
Editorial Assistant: Natalie Bradley
Design: Bold & Noble
Jacket design: Bold & Noble
Assistant Production Manager: Caroline Alberti

ACKNOWLEDGEMENTS

This book is dedicated to my wife, Alexandra,
and my special boy, Joshua.

I would like to thank my mother, Gill, and father, John, for encouraging me into the baking trade in the first place and for washing endless mountains of chef's whites. I'd also like to thank my mother-in-law, Gloria, for helping me with some great recipe ideas.

Above all, a special thank you to my wife, Alexandra, for her support, love and patience during my career and the writing of this book.

CONTENTS

INTRODUCTION

8

Bread is the one natural food that has been with us for centuries, but in recent years it has taken a back seat while we indulged our passion for fast foods bursting with additives and E numbers.

I grew up in Liverpool, the oldest of three boys, and food to us was just a source of energy. It wasn't until I began to make bread in my father's bakery that I realized that the variations and different types of bread were endless, and that bread was not just the thick, white, sliced stuff to make bacon butties with!

The aroma of freshly baked bread evokes feelings and memories in all of us – a snug kitchen in the winter after school and a still-warm loaf on the table waiting to be smothered in butter and homemade strawberry jam is one of my favourites, but who can resist ciabatta straight from the oven, stuffed with glossy black olives, garlic and fresh coriander? Close your eyes and you're sitting on a vine-covered, sun-drenched terrace, sipping a glass of rich, red wine and surrounded by friends and family.

All the recipes in this book have special memories for me; some are from my childhood and some were discovered during my travels abroad. The textures and flavours all vary greatly, reflecting their origins, and I have added something of myself to all these recipes to make them unique and, I hope, satisfying to recreate.

Baking bread is a very sociable experience – you will find the whole family crowding into your kitchen, drawn by the irresistible fragrance of salmon brioche or a potato and rosemary focaccia. So pull up the chairs, break open a bottle and enjoy the novel experience of eating a home-baked loaf of bread.

Introduction

THE HISTORY OF BREAD

I am a man who has bread in Heliopolis

My bread is in heaven with the Sun God,

My bread is on earth with Keb.

The bark of evening and of morning

Brings me the bread that is my meat

From the house of the Sun God.

BOOK OF THE DEAD, ANCIENT EGYPT

From the depths of time bread has been the one common factor that has linked the world's cultures together.

A recent excavation in Egypt, two miles south of the Sphinx, revealed an ancient bakery complete with moulds and working tools of the day. Meanwhile, in London, builders working along the banks of the River Thames unearthed ancient loaves of bread dating back to Roman times.

The first breads made were dense and unappealing – the grain was crushed and mixed with water to create a gruel, which was then left over a fire to cook hard. They were ideal for early man, being easy to carry on the hunt or into battle, and they would keep for days at a time, but they were not very appetizing.

It was the Ancient Egyptians who took baking ten steps further. They discovered that the crushed grain and water mush, if left in a warm and moist atmosphere, would produce bubbles – the first sign of risen bread. This, mixed with fresh flour and then baked, would produce an aerated bread – and so the first yeast was created. Bread was incredibly important to the Egyptians. The lower classes lived almost exclusively on bread and it was used as a form of payment by the Pharaohs for work done on the pyramids and temples. Today's Egyptians still eat their meat or vegetables stuffed into loaves of bread, rather like a kebab.

The people of Israel were influenced by their contact with the Egyptians and began to produce a bread of their own. Theirs was a nomadic society, so until they settled, they baked their dough in the ashes of fires, producing a flat, cake-like bread. Later on, they began to build ovens and granaries, some of which, like the hill fortress of Masada, are still visible today.

The Greeks began by importing their corn from Egypt, but later began to cultivate their own crops. Grain equalled power in Ancient Greece; landowners were eligible for high offices when a certain standard of productivity was obtained, and in the 7th century BC the 'Party of Bread' – the most prosperous farmers – ruled Athens.

The Roman Empire also imported their flour from overseas, from such places as Egypt and North Africa, and the Romans were responsible for the introduction of the water mill. These entrepreneurs had also developed elegant tastes and many of the breads made then would be acceptable today – sesame seed bread, almond bread and milk bread, to name but a few. After the Roman Empire eventually collapsed, it appears that, even as late as the 5th century, many Europeans were still making their bread at home.

The art of bread making progressed slowly during the Dark Ages, and baking remained a family task in the villages and countryside for many hundreds of years. Eventually, communal ovens were introduced and, for a fee, bakers baked off the bread that was brought in. Some of these communal ovens are still currently in operation in France, where they consider the practice of bread making to be an art form.

Today, there are still people all over the world who bake their bread daily. The Bedouin in Petra, Jordan, bake on a bakestone, the modern version of which is a metal dome, lightly oiled and set over a flame. In some European countries, families still come together to bake bread and make it a social occasion, and some even have specially made ovens in their back gardens for just such an event.

Bread holds a social, religious and gastronomic significance for all of us, but it is not just the act of breaking the bread that we should honour, but also the act of making or creating the bread.

TOOLS, TECHNIQUES & TIPS

TOOLS

There are only a few tools needed to make
a good loaf:

1. Baking trays and loaf tins

Any 450g (1lb) traditional loaf tin is ideal
for making breads. There are several varieties
available, from Teflon to non-stick; some
tins have straight sides, while others, such as
farmhouse tins, tend to be more rounded.

Do remember to grease the tins – I use olive oil
– before putting the dough in as this will ensure
that the bread doesn't stick.

Baking trays are lined throughout – I line my
trays with silicone paper or baking parchment.
Greaseproof paper tends to stick.

2. Ovens

I have made bread in or on every oven imaginable,
from open-flame to fan-assisted to range cookers;
all are great for baking bread. Every oven has a
character, especially in professional bakeries,
and hot spots are common. Be aware of your
oven as it may have these elusive hot spots; use
them when baking and remember to turn your
bread if the oven is a little hot at the back – the
main reason for ovens being especially hot at the
back is because over-impatient bakers look in
the oven too often.

Most of the recipes in this book need oven
temperatures between 200–220°C/400–425°F/
gas mark 6–7. This is more than enough heat
to bake bread. Most industrial bakeries bake
at 250°C/475°F/gas mark 9+, the main reason
being to keep moisture in the loaf. The longer
a loaf takes to colour or bake, the drier it will be.

3. A good serrated knife or a sharp blade

I have no preferences with the knives that I use
– any will do, but just remember to keep them
sharp: the cut on the bread is very important,
not only for the look, but for the crumb texture.

TECHNIQUES

Yeast

There are two main types of yeast available in the
supermarkets today – dried and instant. Using
dried yeast makes more work for yourself because
you have to add water and sugar and leave it to
froth. Instant yeast is more user-friendly because
you literally throw it straight into the flour.
However, be aware that this is a concentrated
yeast and you will need less of it. All the recipes
in this book use fresh yeast, but I would suggest
you use instant yeast if you can't obtain fresh –
if you use instant or dried, then use 25 per cent
less than the recipe states. Fresh yeast is available
from most supermarkets nowadays – ask at the
bakery counter for a small amount and more
often than not they will sell it to you. Failing that,
ask at your local bakery.

Remember: all recipes use fresh yeast, so if you are using instant or dried yeast, reduce the quantities by 25 per cent.

Mixing the ingredients for the dough

When mixing the ingredients, avoid contact between the yeast and salt: salt kills yeast, which means the bread won't rise.

Kneading

Kneading is an important part of bread making. The way I knead is very simple: start by making an indentation with the palms of your hands into the middle of the dough – not too deep – then lift up the dough at the top and press it into the hole you have just made. Turn the dough and repeat, and keep repeating this process for the length of time stated in the recipe. The kneading times I give may fluctuate by 2 minutes either way as you get more proficient.

Adding flavourings to the dough

Always add any flavourings after the dough has been kneaded and rested for at least 1 hour as this helps the dough to stabilize before being pumped with any additions.

When adding ingredients such as onions and garlic – ingredients that are intrinsically acidic – do not add too much as this retards or slows down the rising of the dough.

TIPS

- Use this book as a base, but try incorporating your own ingredients and experiment with flavours and textures.

- You do not always need to dissolve yeast in warm water, just lob it in.

- You do not always need to use warm water when making bread, the bread will rise anyway, even in the fridge. The slower the rising (proving) time, the more flavour the bread will have.

- The recipes in this book have measured water contents, but flours differ, so you may need a little extra or a little less water.

- When rolling out and kneading the dough, do not coat the table in inches of flour. The dough will pick it up and tighten up too much.

- I do not normally cover the dough when it is resting; a little skinning on the top should be incorporated back into the dough.

- Always preheat your oven so that your bread has somewhere to go when it is ready.

- None of the breads in this book require steam or pots of water in the oven. I like the crusty earthy look of home-baked bread – there's nothing better.

- I put most of my breads onto a wire rack when they come out of the oven – this is to prevent the bread from sweating and going soft.

- Do not store baked bread in the fridge – it will go stale 3 times quicker than if left in a bread bin.

WHEATSHEAF LOAF

To help you with the skills needed to make bread, your first task is to make a wheatsheaf loaf, which is a display bread and is pictured on page 9. If you can make a wheatsheaf you can make anything in this book. Before you begin, read the tips on the previous pages.

750g (1lb 10oz) strong white
  flour, plus extra for dusting
60g (2¼oz) salt
5g (⅛oz) fresh yeast
60ml (2fl oz) olive oil
420ml (15fl oz) water
1 egg, beaten, for eggwash

I

Put the flour in a bowl about 30.5cm/12 inches in diameter, then add the salt to the left and the yeast to the right. This is to avoid contact between the yeast and the salt (remember, salt kills yeast on contact, which means the bread won't rise). Although you do not need to avoid contact between the two when making a wheatsheaf, it is a good practice to get into.

2

Add the olive oil and slowly start to add the water. (It's not necessary to use virgin olive oil since a lot of the flavour of the oil will be lost during baking.)

3

Begin squeezing the mixture together in your hands. The aim is to pick up all the flour in the bowl with the water – you may need a little extra or a little less water. What you are looking for is a soft, pliable dough.

4

Now shape the dough roughly into a ball and tip it out onto a lightly floured surface. (I say lightly floured because most people make the fatal error of adding too much flour, tightening up the dough too much, and what started as a perfect dough ends up like a brick.)

5

Now you can begin kneading (*see* page 13). Turn the dough 45 degrees and make another indentation and fold in the top of the dough. Repeat this process for 10 minutes. With practice you will eventually get quicker. Put the dough back in the bowl to rest for 1 hour. This is to allow the dough to relax and the yeast to activate.

6

Rip off about a quarter of the dough and, using a rolling pin, roll it out to a rectangle about 45.5cm/18 inches long and 1cm/½ inch thick – use a little flour to stop the rolling pin from attaching itself to the dough.

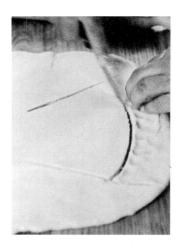  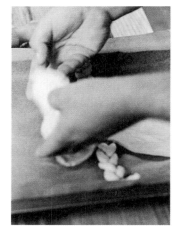

7

Using a knife, cut out a
keyhole, or wheatsheaf,
shape from the dough, about
45.5cm/18 inches long and
20.5cm/8 inches across at the
top, round end. Using the
dough trimmings and extra
dough, hand-roll out 20–30
pieces about 20.5cm/8 inches
long and as thin as you can get
them. (When rolling dough,
the trick is to use the full
length of your hand, from your
fingertips to your palms.)

8

To plait the dough, spread three
strands in front of you and join
them at the top. Cross the left
strand over the middle one to
the right and the right strand
over the middle one to the
left, then repeat until you have
plaited the whole length.

9

Line a baking tray with silicone
paper and put the keyhole
dough on it. Carefully raise the
round end of the wheatsheaf
dough and place the plait under
it at the bottom, with the excess
laid out on either side. Press
firmly to flatten out the dough
underneath.

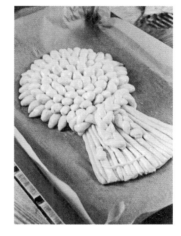

10

Brush the straight length with a little water, then begin adding the hand-rolled strands from the top of the straight length down to the bottom, to simulate the stems of the corn. When the base is covered, trim off any overhanging bits at the bottom, reroll them and use to make a long-tailed mouse. Place the mouse towards the bottom of the stems of corn.

11

Next, rip off small pieces of dough and roll into balls, then slightly elongate them. Brush the round head of the dough with a little water. Place a row of balls to just overlap the top edge of the strips on the straight length, then add a row above. Fold in the two ends of the plait onto where the strips of dough meet the balls and press lightly to seal. Place balls all around the edge of the round head, then fill in the centre with rows of balls just overlapping the previous row. Leave the wheatsheaf to rest for 1 hour, to allow it to rise slightly.

12

Preheat the oven to 200°C/400°F/gas mark 6. Brush the wheatsheaf with the eggwash – this will give the baked bread a beautiful golden shine – and bake for 30 minutes. Reduce the temperature to 150°C/300°F/ gas mark 2 and bake for 30 minutes more. Cool on a wire rack.

BASIC
BREADS

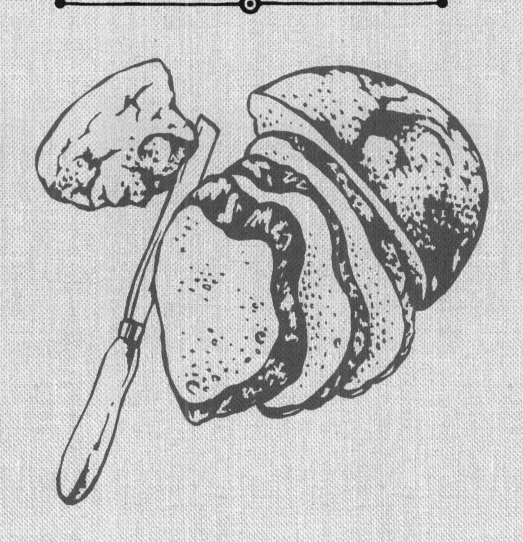

WHITE BREAD

Remember to use a little olive oil to grease your loaf tin. Apply it using a cloth or spray gun.

500g (1lb 2oz) strong white flour,
  plus extra for dusting
10g (⅓oz) salt
60ml (2fl oz) olive oil
15g (½oz) yeast
270ml (9½fl oz) water

MAKES I LOAF

Mix all the ingredients in a large bowl, taking care not to put the yeast on top of the salt. Turn out onto a lightly floured surface. Knead well with your hands and knuckles, then put the dough back in the bowl and leave to rise for 1 hour.

Oil a 450g (1lb) loaf tin. Tip the dough out onto a lightly floured surface and mould into a sausage shape. Put in the tin and leave to rise for 30 minutes–1 hour.

Preheat the oven to 230°C/450°F/gas mark 8. Dust the top of the dough with flour and bake for 25–30 minutes.

Take out of the oven and turn the loaf out onto a wire rack to cool.

CRUSTY COB

This bread, which dates back to medieval times, was known as one of the oven bottoms, as this was invariably where it was baked (as is the Farl on page 31). Baked to a deep colour, it's a great British loaf – I remember watching my dad moulding these when I was a kid.

500g (1lb 2oz) strong white flour,
  plus extra for dusting
10g (⅓oz) salt
15g (½oz) yeast
40g (1½oz) butter, softened
300ml (½ pint) water

MAKES I LOAF

Put the flour, salt, yeast and butter into a large bowl and mix together. Add *almost* all the water and blend the ingredients together, then add the remaining water and mix in the bowl for 2 minutes.

Tip the dough out onto a lightly floured surface and knead well for 5 minutes, then place the dough back in the bowl and leave to rest for 2 hours.

Line a baking tray. Shape the dough into a ball, place on the baking tray and leave to rise for 1 hour.

Preheat the oven to 220°C/425°F/gas mark 7. Using a sharp knife, slash the dough across the top and dust with flour. Bake for 25–30 minutes until golden brown, then transfer to a wire rack to cool.

Basic Breads

BATCH BREAD

A very old British recipe, mainly baked around Georgian times when white flour was prevalent. This sweet white loaf was favoured by the upper crust of this country!

500g (1lb 2oz) strong white flour,
  plus extra for dusting
10g (⅓oz) salt
20g (¾oz) yeast
60g (2¼oz) butter, softened
75g (3oz) caster sugar
300ml (½ pint) water

MAKES 1 LOAF

Put all the ingredients into a large bowl and mix together. When all the flour has been picked up by the water, tip the dough out onto a lightly floured surface and knead for 5 minutes. If you find the dough sticks to the table a lot, then dust lightly again with flour, but do not over-flour as this will tighten the dough. Put the dough back in the bowl and leave to rest for 1 hour.

Line a baking tray. Tip the dough out onto a floured surface and shape into a ball, then gently flatten it out with your hand until it is about 20.5cm/8 inches in diameter. Place on the baking tray, dust the top with flour and leave to rise for 1–2 hours.

Preheat the oven to 200°C/400°F/gas mark 6. Bake for 15–20 minutes, then transfer to a wire rack to cool.

WHITE/WHOLEMEAL TIN BREAD

The ubiquitous loaf the Brits have brought to the table. But I shouldn't mock! Made well, this is a beautiful bread – served as toast or as a simple sandwich it's magic! The main recipe is for white bread, but try the wholemeal version to help you understand the different textures.

500g (1lb) strong white flour,
  plus extra for dusting
10g (⅓oz) salt
20g (¾oz) yeast
50g (1¾oz) butter, softened
290ml (10fl oz) water

MAKES 1 LARGE LOAF OR 2 SMALL LOAVES

Put the flour, salt, yeast and butter into a bowl, then add the water, little by little, folding in with your hands until all the flour has been picked up. Tip out onto a lightly floured surface and knead for 5 minutes until you have a pliable, soft dough. Put the dough back in the bowl and leave for 1 hour.

Oil a 900g (2lb) loaf tin or two 450g (1lb) loaf tins. Shape the dough to fit the tin(s), and leave to rise for 1 hour.

Preheat the oven to 230°C/450°F/gas mark 8. Just before you bake the loaf, dust the top with flour and, using a knife, make slashes across the top. Bake for 30–35 minutes for the large tin or 20–25 minutes if using smaller tins. Then turn out of the tin(s) onto a wire rack to cool.

Variation: For Wholemeal Tin Bread, use 400g (14oz) wholemeal flour and 100g (3½oz) white flour instead of the 500g (1lb 2oz) white flour, and use 325ml (11fl oz) water. Proceed as above.

BASIC WHOLEMEAL BREAD

Wholemeal flour does take more water than white flour. If you find that your particular flour needs more water than the quantity given, then by all means add more. Make the dough quite wet, because as the dough rests it does tighten up.

100g (3½oz) strong white flour,
  plus extra for dusting
400g (14oz) wholemeal flour
10g (⅓oz) salt
20g (¾oz) yeast
50g (1¾oz) butter, softened
350ml (12fl oz) water

MAKES 1 LOAF

Put the flours, salt, yeast and butter into a large bowl and mix together. Slowly add the water, mixing with your hand until all the flour has been incorporated from the sides of the bowl.

Tip the dough out onto a lightly floured surface and knead for 5–7 minutes. Put the dough back in the bowl and leave to rest for 1 hour.

Line a baking tray, mould the dough into a sausage shape and place on the baking tray. Leave to rise for 30–45 minutes.

Preheat the oven to 220°C/425°F/gas mark 7. Dust the top of the dough with flour, then use a knife to cut a slash down the middle on top of the loaf. Bake for 30 minutes, then transfer to a wire rack to cool.

COTTAGE LOAF

This bread is a very British shape. It originated some time around the 1500s and still exists in small village bakeries around the country.

400g (14oz) strong white flour,
  plus extra for dusting
10g (⅓oz) salt
20g (¾oz) yeast
60g (2¼oz) butter, softened
250ml (9fl oz) water

MAKES 1 LOAF

Put all the ingredients into a bowl and mix until you have a soft, pliable dough.

Tip the dough out onto a lightly floured surface and knead with your fingers for 5 minutes, then put back in the bowl and leave to rest for 1 hour.

Preheat the oven to 230°C/450°F/gas mark 8. Line a baking tray. Tip the dough out onto a floured surface, rip off a third of the dough and shape into a ball. Shape the remaining dough into a ball and place on the baking tray. Put the smaller ball on top of the larger one, then flatten slightly with your hand. Push your finger down through the centre of the loaf from top to bottom until you can feel the table. Dust the loaf with flour and, using a knife, make vertical slashes from the top of the loaf to the bottom (be careful not to cut yourself).

Leave to rise for 30 minutes, then bake for 30 minutes until golden brown. Transfer to a wire rack to cool.

When cooled, serve with chunks of cheese.

NAMED BREAD

A friend started me on this – it was his birthday and he asked me if he could see his name in bread – better than in lights!

These baked letters are for display only.

500g (1lb 2oz) strong white flour,
  plus extra for dusting
50g (1¾oz) salt
5g (⅛oz) yeast
30ml (1fl oz) olive oil
270ml (9½fl oz) water
1 egg, beaten, for eggwash
Wood varnish, to glaze

MAKES 400 SMALL LETTERS

Put all the ingredients into a bowl and mix well by rubbing in. Tip the dough out onto a lightly floured surface and knead for 6 minutes, then put the dough back in the bowl to rest for 1 hour.

Line several baking trays. Divide the dough into however many letters you require, e.g. Paul needs 4, so cut 4 x 100 pieces of dough, and shape the dough into the required letters. Put the letters on the baking tray so they are just touching, and leave to rest for 1 hour.

Preheat the oven to 220°C/425°F/gas mark 7. Brush the letters liberally with the eggwash and bake for 30–40 minutes until they are a strong dark brown colour.

Transfer to a wire rack to cool. The next day, coat the names with wood varnish to preserve them.

MILK LOAF

A very ancient bread. Milk has been used in bread for at least 1,500 years and it gives a characteristic flavour and a fairly tight texture.

500g (1lb 2oz) strong white flour,
  plus extra for dusting
5g (⅛oz) salt
50g (1¾oz) caster sugar
60g (2¼oz) butter, softened
25g (1oz) yeast
300ml (½ pint) milk

MAKES 2 LOAVES

Put all the ingredients into a large bowl. Using a mixer, begin blending slowly, then speed up as you start to pick up all the flour. Alternatively, mix by hand.

Tip the dough out onto a lightly floured surface and knead for 5 minutes. Put the dough back in the bowl and leave to rise for about 1 hour, or until doubled in size.

Tip the dough out onto a floured surface and divide into two equal pieces. Shape each piece roughly into a sausage shape and place crease-side down into two 450g (1lb) loaf tins. Leave to rise for 1 hour.

Preheat the oven to 200°C/400°F/gas mark 6. Bake for 25–30 minutes until golden brown, then turn out onto a wire rack to cool.

DARK RYE BREAD

This earthy, hearty, full-flavoured loaf is from Eastern Europe. It will take up to 30 per cent more water than most bread doughs. The recipe uses rye baskets – they can be bought in basketware shops or ordered through the Internet. ILLUSTRATED

350g (12oz) dark rye flour,
  plus extra for dusting
150g (5½oz) wholemeal flour
5g (⅛oz) salt
20g (¾oz) yeast
4 tablespoons malt extract
2 tablespoons treacle
325ml (11fl oz) water
2 teaspoons cumin seeds

MAKES 2 SMALL LOAVES

Put 175g (6oz) of the rye flour and 75g (3oz) of the wholemeal flour into a bowl, then stir in the salt, yeast, malt extract and treacle along with 150ml (¼ pint) of water. Mix well for 5 minutes, then leave in the bowl to rise for 5 hours.

Line a baking tray. Add the remaining flours and water and the cumin seeds to the dough and mix well. Tip out onto a lightly floured surface, divide the dough into two equal pieces and shape each into an oblong sausage. Coat each sausage with rye flour, place each in a rye basket and leave to rise for 2–3 hours.

Preheat the oven to 220°C/425°F/gas mark 7. Tip each loaf out onto the baking tray and bake for 25–30 minutes, then transfer to a wire rack to cool.

IRISH SODA BREAD

I've tweaked this recipe over the years and am finally proud of it. It's gorgeous served fresh from the oven with lots of butter.

500g (1lb 2oz) strong white flour,
  plus extra for dusting
20g (¾oz) baking powder
1 teaspoon salt
75g (3oz) butter, softened
150ml (¼ pint) buttermilk
200ml (7fl oz) milk

MAKES 2 LOAVES

Put the flour, baking powder and salt into a bowl and work in the butter. Stir in the remaining ingredients and mix well.

Line a baking tray. Combine the mixture with your hands to make a dough, then divide the dough into two equal pieces and shape into balls. Flatten the balls out and cut crosses in the top of each, then put on the baking tray and leave to rest for 20 minutes.

Preheat the oven to 200°C/400°F/gas mark 6. Dust the dough lightly with flour and bake for 25–30 minutes. Transfer to a wire rack to cool.

WHOLEMEAL SODA BREAD

I first ate this bread, baked for me by monks, while staying in Roscrea Monastery in Ireland.
ILLUSTRATED

250g (9oz) strong white flour,
  plus extra for dusting
250g (9oz) wholemeal flour
20g (¾oz) baking powder
1 teaspoon salt
75g (3oz) butter, softened
270ml (9½fl oz) milk
30ml (1fl oz) buttermilk

MAKES 1 LOAF

Preheat the oven to 200°C/400°F/gas mark 6. Line a baking tray. Put all the ingredients into a large bowl and work together to form a soft dough, adding a dash more milk if necessary. Shape into a ball and flatten slightly, then dust the top with a little flour and cut a cross into the top.

Put onto the baking tray and bake for 30–35 minutes until golden brown. Transfer to a wire rack to cool.

Variation: This bread can be made with 100 per cent white flour – just replace the wholemeal flour with 250g (9oz) white flour. Proceed as above.

CHEESE & ONION SODA BREAD

A nice twist on the traditional bread, and tastes fantastic!

500g (1lb 2oz) strong white flour,
  plus extra for dusting
1 teaspoon salt
300ml (½ pint) buttermilk
100ml (3½fl oz) milk
75g (3oz) butter, softened
20g (¾oz) baking powder
1 onion, peeled and finely chopped
75g (3oz) Cheddar cheese, grated

MAKES 2 LOAVES

Preheat the oven to 220°C/425°F/gas mark 7. Line a baking tray. Put all the ingredients except the onion and cheese in a food mixer and, using a paddle blade and medium speed, blend together for 2 minutes. Alternatively, put into a bowl and mix well by hand for 5 minutes. Add the onion and cheese and incorporate, either by hand or in the mixer (don't overmix), into the dough.

Divide the dough into two equal pieces and tip out onto a lightly floured surface. Shape each piece into a ball, then flatten with your hand so they are approximately 5cm/2 inches thick. Dust the loaves with a little flour, cut a deep cross into each and put on the baking tray.

Bake for 20–25 minutes and serve warm.

BEER BREAD

Not that I drink a lot of beer (I prefer lager), but this bread is delicious! Serve with a good mature Cheddar cheese.

250g (9oz) wholemeal flour
250g (9oz) strong white flour,
  plus extra for dusting
10g (⅓oz) salt
20g (¾oz) yeast
30g (1oz) butter, softened
300ml (½ pint) good strong beer

MAKES I LOAF

Put all the ingredients into a bowl and mix until all the flour has been picked up. Tip the dough out onto a lightly floured surface and knead for 5 minutes until the dough is smooth and creamy. Put the dough back in the bowl to rest for 1 hour.

Line a baking tray. Tip the dough out onto a floured surface and shape into a ball on the baking tray, then flatten out with your hands. Cut diagonal lines across the top. Leave to rise for 1 hour.

Preheat the oven to 200°C/400°F/gas mark 6. Bake for 30 minutes until golden brown, then transfer to a wire rack to cool.

GUINNESS & TREACLE BREAD

Another hearty loaf, with a little extra iron (i.e. Guinness). Eat yourself fit!

350g (12oz) wholemeal flour,
  plus extra for dusting
150g (5½oz) strong white flour,
  plus extra for dusting
10g (⅓oz) salt
20g (¾oz) yeast
2 tablespoons treacle
200ml (7fl oz) Guinness
120ml (4fl oz) water

MAKES I LOAF

Put all the ingredients into a large bowl and mix together for a few minutes. Tip the dough out onto a lightly floured surface and knead for 5 minutes, then put the dough back in the bowl and leave to rest for 1 hour.

Line a baking tray. Tip the dough out onto a floured surface and shape into a ball, then flatten out to a 25.5cm/10 inch round and roll up. Put the dough on the baking tray and leave to rise for 1 hour.

Preheat the oven to 200°C/400°F/gas mark 6. Cut several slashes across the bread and dust with wholemeal flour. Bake for 30 minutes, then transfer to a wire rack to cool.

STILTON & BACON BREAD

This bread is an old favourite of mine, originally created for the Michelin-starred restaurant at The Dorchester. Serve as a sandwich, piled high with crisp green salad, roasted red and yellow peppers, and slivers of mustard-roasted beef. You need to start this the day before.

500g (1lb 2oz) strong white flour,
  plus extra for dusting
360ml (12½fl oz) water
20g (¾oz) yeast
1 teaspoon salt
75g (3oz) Stilton cheese, crumbled
125g (4½oz) bacon, chopped and fried

MAKES 2 LOAVES

Put 125g (4½oz) of the flour, 120ml (4fl oz) of the water and 15g (½oz) of the yeast into a bowl and mix together by hand, then whisk with a hand whisk for 5 minutes. Leave to rise in a warm place overnight.

The dough will now smell fermented, rather like beer. Add the remaining flour, water and yeast along with the salt and knead well for 5 minutes, then leave to rest for 30 minutes.

Line a baking tray. Tip the dough out onto a lightly floured surface and knead in the Stilton and bacon, then cut the dough in half and shape into two rounds. Put on the baking tray and leave to prove for 1 hour.

Preheat the oven to 200°C/400°F/gas mark 6. Dust the loaves with flour and bake for 30 minutes, then transfer to a wire rack to cool.

MULTI-FLAVOURED BREAD

This multi-flavoured and coloured bread is ideal for indecisive families – there are rolls of four flavours in each loaf. It's great for dinner parties, too. The dough can be frozen when made, if not using immediately, and then defrosted overnight before baking.

½ quantity Curried Naan Bread dough
  (*see* page 73)
½ quantity Date & Fig Bread dough
  (*see* page 104)
½ quantity Pepper & Onion Flowerpot
  Bread dough (*see* page 88)
½ quantity Stilton & Walnut Wholemeal
  Loaf dough (*see* page 103)
Milk, to glaze

FOR THE TOPPINGS
Sesame seeds
Poppy seeds
Flour
Grated cheese

MAKES 4 SMALL LOAVES

Line two baking trays. Make the doughs and divide them into twenty-four 100g (3½oz) pieces, then shape them into balls.

Place one ball of dough on the tray and surround with five balls of different flavours. Make similar circles with the remaining balls, then leave to rise for 1 hour. The individual circles of dough will join up to form loaves. Brush the tops of the loaves with milk and sprinkle with the toppings.

Preheat the oven to 200°C/400°F/gas mark 6. Bake for 25 minutes, then transfer to a wire rack to cool. Et voilà – multi flavours!

FARL

This bread is a very English loaf, traditionally baked on the bottom of the oven, hence its other name: oven bottoms!

500g (1lb 2oz) strong white flour,
  plus extra for dusting
10g (⅓oz) salt
30g (1oz) yeast
60g (2¼oz) butter, softened
300ml (½ pint) water

MAKES 1 LARGE LOAF

Put all the ingredients into a bowl and mix for 4 minutes. Tip out onto a lightly floured surface and knead for 5 minutes until the dough is smooth and pliable. Leave in the bowl to rise for 1 hour.

Line a baking tray. Tip the dough out onto a floured surface and shape into a ball, then flatten into a circle about 5cm/2 inches thick. Put on the baking tray and leave to rise for 1 hour.

Preheat the oven to 220°C/425°F/gas mark 7. Cover the top of the dough with flour and, starting from the middle, make vertical slashes down the dough all the way round. Bake for 30 minutes, then transfer to a wire rack to cool.

SCONES

A traditional afternoon tea favourite, served with clotted cream and strawberry jam. I've worked in several five-star hotels and, as far as I'm concerned, afternoon tea is the best snack of the day – especially at Cliveden. ILLUSTRATED

500g (1lb 2oz) strong white flour,
  plus extra for dusting
2 medium eggs, beaten, plus
  1 egg, beaten, for eggwash
75g (3oz) caster sugar
30g (1oz) baking powder
75g (3oz) butter, softened
225ml (8fl oz) milk
100g (3½oz) sultanas

MAKES 15–18 SCONES

Preheat the oven to 220°C/425°F/gas mark 7. Line a baking tray.

Put all the ingredients, except the eggwash and sultanas, into a food mixer and, using a paddle blade, mix for about 2 minutes on slow speed. If mixing by hand this will take about 5 minutes.

Incorporate the sultanas into the dough and tip out onto a lightly floured surface. Using a rolling pin, roll out the dough to about 3–4cm/1¼–1½ inches thick, then, using a round cutter, cut out the scones. (I normally use a 5–7.5cm/2–3 inch cutter for hotel-size scones.)

Put the scones on the baking tray and brush with the eggwash. If you have time, chill the eggwashed scones in the fridge for 30 minutes before baking to help with a straight rise.

Remove the scones from the fridge and brush the tops again with eggwash, being careful not to let it dribble down the sides as this will hinder their rise in the oven. Bake for 15 minutes, then transfer to a wire rack to cool a little. Serve warm.

Basic Breads

WHOLEMEAL SCONES

These are a particular favourite of a friend of mine, Chris Davies, who insisted I put the recipe in the book. If preferred you may add 50g (1¾oz) sultanas to the dough when it has been formed.

250g (9oz) strong white flour,
  plus extra for dusting
250g (9oz) wholemeal flour
75g (3oz) caster sugar
30g (1oz) baking powder
75g (3oz) butter, softened
2 medium eggs, beaten, plus
  1 egg, beaten, for eggwash
270ml (9½fl oz) milk

MAKES 15–18 SCONES

Preheat the oven to 200°C/400°F/gas mark 6. Line a baking tray.

Put the flours, sugar and baking powder into a large bowl and mix together.

Add the butter, eggs and milk and, using your hands, mix together thoroughly for 6 minutes.

Turn the dough out onto a lightly floured surface and, using a rolling pin, flatten it to about 3–4cm/1¼–1½ inches thick. Using a round cutter (any size you like – I prefer to use 5–7.5cm/2–3 inch cutters), cut out the scones.

Put the scones on the baking tray and brush with the eggwash. If you have time, chill the eggwashed scones in the fridge for 30 minutes before baking to help with a straight rise.

Remove the scones from the fridge and brush the tops again with eggwash, being careful not to let it dribble down the sides as this will hinder their rise in the oven. Bake for 15–20 minutes until golden brown, then transfer to a wire rack to cool a little. Serve with strawberry jam.

CHEESE SCONES

Cheese and scones are a marriage made in heaven. You can add 30g (1oz) sultanas to the dough if you like.

500g (1lb 2oz) strong white flour,
  plus extra for dusting
30g (1oz) caster sugar
30g (1oz) baking powder
75g (3oz) butter, softened
2 eggs, beaten together, plus
  1 egg, beaten, for eggwash
240ml (8½fl oz) milk
100g (3½oz) Cheddar cheese, grated

MAKES 15 SCONES

Line a baking tray. Put the flour, sugar, baking powder, butter, the 2 beaten eggs and the milk into a bowl, and bring together gently with your hands. When the dough has formed, add most of the cheese (reserving a little for sprinkling) and mix again for 5 minutes.

Tip the dough out onto a lightly floured surface and knead gently for 4 minutes until the dough is smooth. Roll out the dough to 4cm/1½ inches thick and, using a round cutter of your choice, cut out the scones. Put the scones on the baking tray, brush the tops with the eggwash and put in the fridge for 30 minutes (this helps the scones to rise up straight).

Preheat the oven to 220°C/425°F/gas mark 7. Remove the scones from the fridge and brush the tops again with eggwash, being careful not to let it dribble down the sides as this will hinder their rise in the oven. Sprinkle a little cheese onto each scone and bake for 15 minutes until golden brown. Transfer to a wire rack to cool.

CHEESE BISCUITS

These biscuits can be served as a snack or with cheese at the end of a meal. Any cheese goes well with them – they're great.

375g (13oz) strong white flour,
  plus extra for dusting
1 teaspoon salt
125g (4½oz) butter, softened
40ml (1½fl oz) water
2 medium eggs, beaten in separate bowls

FOR THE FLAVOURINGS
1) 2 tablespoons poppy seeds
2) 40g (1½oz) Gruyère cheese
3) 2 teaspoons caraway seeds

MAKES 30–40 THIN BISCUITS

Put the flour, salt, butter, water and 1 beaten egg into a bowl, and mix well for 5 minutes.

Divide the dough into three equal pieces, and add the poppy seeds to one, the Gruyère to the second, and the caraway seeds to the third. Wrap each piece in clingfilm and chill for 2 hours.

Preheat the oven to 220°C/425°F/gas mark 7. Line a baking tray. Using a rolling pin, roll out each piece of dough on a lightly floured surface to about 3mm/⅛ inch thick. Using a round cutter of your choice (I use a 7.5cm/3 inch cutter), cut out the dough. Place the discs on the baking tray and brush with the remaining beaten egg.

Bake for 15 minutes until golden brown, then transfer to a wire rack to cool. Serve warm or cold.

MIXED ROLLS

These rolls are great for dinner parties – with three flavours to choose from, there's one to appeal to everyone.

FOR THE DOUGH

500g (1lb 2oz) strong white flour, plus extra for dusting
10g (⅓oz) salt
60g (2¼oz) butter, softened
20g (¾oz) yeast
300ml (½ pint) water

FOR THE FLAVOURINGS

1) **20g (¾oz) red or green peppers, deseeded and finely chopped, and 20g (¾oz) onion, peeled and finely chopped**
2) **20g (¾oz) Stilton cheese, crumbled, and 30g (1oz) chopped walnuts**
3) **75g (3oz) firm Brie cheese, chopped, and a good handful of freshly chopped basil**

MAKES 12 ROLLS

Put all the ingredients for the dough into a bowl and mix until all the flour has been picked up. Tip the dough out onto a lightly floured surface and knead for 5 minutes, then put the dough back in the bowl and leave to rest for 1 hour.

Line two baking trays and dust with a little flour. Divide the dough into three equal pieces. Incorporate the peppers and onion into one piece, then quarter the dough. Shape the quarters into balls, place on a baking tray, then cut a cross on the top of each one.

Incorporate the Stilton and walnuts into the second piece of dough, then quarter the dough. Roll each piece into a long, thin sausage and tie in a knot, then place on a baking tray.

Roll out the remaining piece of dough into a 20 x 13cm/8 x 5 inches rectangle and scatter the top with the Brie and basil. Starting from the short side, roll up the rectangle and press lightly on the edge to seal. Cut into four and place each piece, cut-side down, on a baking tray. Leave all the rolls to rise for 1 hour.

Preheat the oven to 220°C/425°F/gas mark 7. Bake for 15–20 minutes, then transfer to a wire rack to cool.

FRENCH BREADS

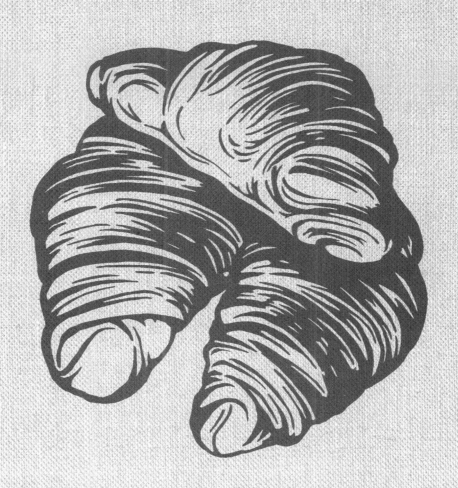

PAIN DE CAMPAGNE

*The French are passionate about their bread –
historically, the shaving of bakers' heads for selling
underweight bread was not uncommon. This loaf
typifies French bread – a big, bold, hearty loaf full of
flavour. Serve toasted or with cheese, it's a must-try!*
ILLUSTRATED

400g (14oz) strong white flour,
  plus extra for dusting
100g (3½oz) rye flour
10g (⅓oz) salt
20g (¾oz) yeast
50g (1¾oz) butter, softened
Large bunch of fresh oregano,
  destalked and chopped
300ml (½pint) water

MAKES 1 LOAF

Put all the ingredients, except the water, into a
bowl, then slowly add the water and mix in with
your hands until all the flour on the sides of the
bowl has been incorporated.

Tip the dough out onto a lightly floured surface
and knead for 6 minutes. Put the dough back in
the bowl and leave for 2 hours.

Line a baking tray. Tip the dough out onto a
floured surface and shape into a ball, then slightly
flatten with your hands and dust with flour.
Using a knife, mark out a square shape on top
of the dough, put on the baking tray and leave
to rise for 1 hour.

Preheat the oven to 220°C/425°F/gas mark 7.
Bake for 30 minutes until golden brown, then
transfer to a wire rack to cool.

BAGUETTES

*The ubiquitous baguette, filled with cheese and
ham and then toasted, is my lunch any day. Serve
with a glass of chilled Chablis. Start this bread the
day before.*

500g (1lb 2oz) strong white flour
20g (¾oz) yeast
270ml (9½fl oz) warm water
10g (⅓oz) salt
50g (1¾oz) butter, softened

MAKES 2 BAGUETTES

Mix 200g (7oz) of the flour with all the yeast
and 200ml (7fl oz) of warm water to make
a thick batter, then cover loosely and leave
to rise overnight.

Add the remaining flour, the salt and butter
to the dough, and slowly add enough of the
remaining water to make a soft, pliable dough.
Rest the dough for 1 hour.

Line a baking tray. Bang the air out of the dough
and cut in half. Roll each half into a baguette
shape about 35cm/13¾ inches long. Put on the
baking tray and leave to prove for 1 hour.

Preheat the oven to 220°C/425°F/gas mark 7.
Use a sharp knife to make slashes along the length
of the baguettes. Bake for 20–25 minutes, then
transfer to a wire rack to cool.

ONION & BACON FOUGASSES

This is a traditional French bread, flat and leaf-shaped, very much like the focaccia of Italy. It's eaten with cheese and salads. There are many flavours that go well in this style of bread – try peppers, ham, Cheddar cheese or plain basil – c'est bon!

400g (14oz) strong white flour
20g (¾oz) yeast
200ml (7fl oz) water
1 teaspoon salt
75ml (2½fl oz) olive oil
1 onion, peeled, finely chopped and fried until translucent
3 rashers of back bacon, finely chopped and fried

MAKES 3 FOUGASSES

Line three baking trays. Put 200g (7oz) of the flour with all the yeast and about 175ml (6fl oz) of water into a bowl and beat together for about 3 minutes into a thick batter. Leave to rise and fall – this should take 3–4 hours.

Add the remaining flour and water along with the salt, 60ml (2fl oz) of the olive oil, the fried onion and bacon, and knead well for 5 minutes. Put back in the bowl and leave to rise for 1 hour.

Divide the dough into three equal pieces. Using a rolling pin, flatten each piece into a circle roughly 22cm/8½ inches in diameter. Using a knife, make a slash down the middle of each circle and three diagonal slashes on each side, opening the slashes slightly with your fingers. Place on the baking trays, brush lightly with the remaining olive oil and leave to rise for 1 hour.

Preheat the oven to 230°C/450°F/gas mark 8. Bake for 15 minutes until golden brown, then transfer to a wire rack to cool.

BRIE & BASIL BREAD

I used to sell this by the truckful on Saturdays from our shop in Canterbury.

500g (1lb 2oz) wholemeal flour, plus extra for dusting
60ml (2fl oz) olive oil
10g (⅓oz) salt
20g (¾oz) yeast
325ml (11fl oz) warm water
100g (3½oz) Brie cheese, thinly sliced
Handful of freshly chopped basil leaves

MAKES 1 LOAF

Put the flour, olive oil and salt into a large bowl and rub the mix together. Dilute the yeast in the water and add to the bowl. Slowly add the yeasty water, mixing with your hand as you do, until all the flour has been incorporated and the dough feels soft to the touch.

Tip the dough out onto a lightly floured surface and knead for 6 minutes until you have a pliable dough. Put back in the bowl and leave to rise for 2 hours.

Line a baking tray. Tip the dough out onto a floured surface and, using your hands, shape into a mini baguette about 30cm/12 inches long, then place on the baking tray. Coat the top with wholemeal flour and make several deep slashes in the dough lengthways down the middle. Push the Brie and basil into the cuts, then rest the dough for 2 hours.

Preheat the oven to 200°C/400°F/gas mark 6. Bake for 25 minutes until golden brown, then transfer to a wire rack to cool.

BRIOCHES À TÊTE

A truly French bread. The immortal line uttered by Marie Antoinette, allegedly, 'Let them eat cake', should have read 'Let them eat brioche', as this was more likely a scenario. You need to start this the day before.

375g (13oz) strong white flour
40g (1½oz) caster sugar
15g (½oz) yeast
1 teaspoon salt
75ml (2½fl oz) milk
3 medium eggs, plus 1 egg, beaten, for eggwash
185g (6½oz) butter, softened
10 paper muffin cases

MAKES 10 BRIOCHES

Put the flour, sugar, yeast, salt, milk and the 3 eggs in a food processor and process, using the blade, for about 5 minutes to a firm, smooth dough. If mixing by hand this will take 8 minutes.

Add the butter to the dough and mix for a further 5 minutes in the mixer or 10 minutes by hand. Put the dough in a bowl, cover and refrigerate overnight.

The dough should now be stiff and easily shaped. Cut the dough into 10 equal pieces and cut a quarter off each piece. Using your hands, shape the quarters and the larger pieces into balls. Put each large ball of dough into a muffin case and brush lightly with the eggwash. Push a smaller ball of dough on top of each one. Leave in a warm place to rise for 1 hour.

Preheat the oven to 200°C/400°F/gas mark 6. Brush the brioches with the eggwash and bake for 15 minutes until golden brown. Transfer to a wire rack to cool.

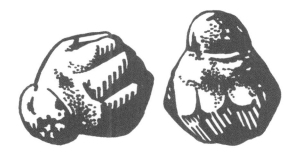

BRIE & BRIOCHE PARCEL

Brioche is rumoured to have been first made around the area where Brie is made, so this is a marriage made in heaven. You need to make the dough the day before. ILLUSTRATED

½ quantity Brioche dough (*see* page 43)
Flour for dusting
250g (9oz) round Brie cheese,
   10cm in diameter
1 egg, beaten, for eggwash

MAKES I PARCEL

Roll out the brioche dough on a lightly floured surface to about 5mm/¼ inch thick and 25cm/10 inches in diameter. Place the cheese in the middle of the dough and fold the sides of the dough neatly onto the middle.

Turn the parcel over so that the joins are underneath, then brush the top with some of the eggwash. Place in the fridge for 1 hour.

Preheat the oven to 200°C/400°F/gas mark 6. Line a baking tray. Place the parcel on the baking tray. Brush with the eggwash again, then, using the back of a knife, score a criss-cross pattern over the parcel. Bake for 15 minutes until golden brown. Serve warm.

SALMON BRIOCHES

During my time at The Dorchester Hotel in London, this brioche was a great favourite of the Sultan of Brunei. It's fabulous when toasted and served on a bed of rocket salad, with a lemon and dill vinaigrette. You need to make the dough the day before.

500g (1lb 2oz) strong white flour,
   plus extra for dusting
5g (⅛oz) salt
50g (1¾oz) caster sugar
6 medium eggs
20g (¾oz) yeast
2 tablespoons milk
250g (9oz) butter, softened
150g (5½oz) smoked salmon, sliced

MAKES 2 BRIOCHES

Put the flour into a bowl with the salt, sugar, eggs and yeast, and gently rub the mixture together. Add the milk, then use your hands to mix the ingredients together for 5 minutes. Leave the dough in a warm place to rest for 30 minutes.

Gradually add the butter to the dough, kneading for a further 6 minutes, then refrigerate the dough overnight. The dough will solidify in the fridge.

Cut the dough into 16 equal pieces. Lightly cover your hands with flour and roll each piece into a small ball. Push your thumb halfway through the middle of each dough ball and place a sliver of salmon inside. Reshape, using a little flour to stop the dough sticking to your hands, and repeat this process until you have 16 mini brioches.

Lightly grease and line two 900g (2lb) loaf tins. Place eight of the balls closely together in each tin and leave to prove for about 1 hour until they have reached three-quarters of the way up the tins.

Preheat the oven to 200°C/400°F/gas mark 6. Bake for 15–20 minutes, then turn out onto a wire rack and leave to cool slightly before serving.

APRICOT BRIOCHES

Brioche is a delicate bread and, stuffed with apricots and toasted, is a full breakfast in itself. You need to start this the day before.

375g (13oz) strong white flour
40g (1½oz) caster sugar
15g (½oz) yeast
Pinch of salt
75ml (2½fl oz) milk
3 medium eggs
185g (6½oz) butter, softened
150g (5½oz) soft, ready-to-eat dried apricots, diced

MAKES 2 BRIOCHES

Put the flour, sugar, yeast, salt, milk and eggs in a food mixer and process, using the blade, for about 5 minutes to a smooth dough. If mixing by hand this will take 8 minutes. Add the butter and mix for a further 5 minutes in a mixer or 10 minutes by hand. Tip the dough out into a bowl, cover and refrigerate overnight.

Grease two 900g (2lb) loaf tins. The dough should now be stiff and easily shaped. Divide the dough into 40g (1½oz) pieces and add 1 teaspoon of the apricots into the middle of each piece. Fold the dough over the filling and shape into little balls. Put the balls in the tins in rows of two balls, one ball, two balls, and so on until the tin is full. Each tin should hold 9–10 pieces. Leave to rise for 1–2 hours.

Preheat the oven to 200°C/400°F/gas mark 6. Bake for 20 minutes until golden brown, then turn out onto a wire rack to cool. Cut into slices, toast and serve with lots of butter.

CROISSANTS

I've included croissants – although not technically a bread – because they are risen with yeast and have become a symbol throughout the world for everything French. Every French pastry chef I've met has claimed he has the best recipe for croissants. I've tried and tested them all and have come to the conclusion that mine are the best! Take a bite and see what you think. You need to start this the day before.

20g (¾oz) yeast
375ml (13fl oz) warm water
625g (1lb 6oz) strong white flour, plus extra for dusting
5g (⅛oz) salt
75g (3oz) caster sugar
500g (1lb 2oz) butter, chilled
1 egg, beaten, for eggwash

MAKES 16 CROISSANTS

Dilute the yeast in the water. Put the flour, salt and sugar into a large mixing bowl. Using a wooden spoon, gradually mix in the yeasty water until the dough becomes pliable. Tip the dough out onto a lightly floured surface and knead well until it feels elastic. Put the dough back in the bowl and refrigerate for 1 hour.

Turn out the chilled dough onto a floured surface and roll it into a 60 x 30.5cm/ 24 x 12 inch rectangle. Flatten the chilled butter between two sheets of clingfilm into a rectangle large enough to cover two-thirds of the dough. Remove the clingfilm and cover two-thirds of the dough with the butter. Bring the uncovered third of the dough into the centre, then fold the covered top third down, so that the dough is now in three layers. Return the dough to the fridge to chill for 1 hour.

Dust the work surface and roll out the dough to the same size rectangle as before. Repeat the folding process, one side on top of the other, and refrigerate for 1 hour. You will need to repeat this process twice more before leaving the dough to rest, wrapped in clingfilm, overnight.

Line three baking trays. Cut the dough in half. Using a rolling pin, roll out each piece into a 40cm/16 inch square. Cut each square into quarters, then cut each quarter diagonally, making two triangles. Lay the triangles on a lightly floured surface with the narrow points away from you, then roll each piece up from the edge nearest you towards the point, ending with the tip underneath. Bend the ends round to make the traditional croissant shape. Put the croissants on the baking trays and leave to rise for 1 hour.

Preheat the oven to 200°C/400°F/gas mark 6. Brush the croissants lightly with the eggwash and bake for 10–15 minutes until golden brown, then transfer to a wire rack to cool.

CHEESE & HAM CROISSANTS

On cold winter nights in the bakery I used to wait patiently for these to come out of the oven, still oozing with cheese. They're great with coffee or as a light snack.

1 quantity Croissant dough (*see* page 48)
1 egg, beaten, for eggwash

FOR THE FILLING
250g (9oz) honey-glazed ham, thinly sliced
200g (7oz) Cheddar cheese, grated

MAKES 16 CROISSANTS

Make the croissant dough as on page 48 up to the point where it is ready to shape. (At this stage you do not have to use all the dough, it can be frozen and will keep for two to three months. To defrost the dough, bring it out of the freezer the night before and thaw overnight.)

Line three baking trays. Cut the dough in half. Using a rolling pin, roll out each piece into a 40cm/16 inch square. Cut each square into quarters, then cut each quarter diagonally, making two triangles. Cut the ham into triangles slightly smaller than the dough, then place on the dough and top with a little grated cheese. Lay the triangles with the narrow points away from you, then roll each triangle up towards the point, ending with the tip underneath. Bend the ends round to make the traditional croissant shape. Put the croissants on the baking trays and leave to rise for 1 hour.

Preheat the oven to 200°C/400°F/gas mark 6. Brush the croissants lightly with the eggwash and bake for 15 minutes until golden brown, then transfer to a wire rack to cool.

PAINS AU CHOCOLAT

*If there is no other recipe in this book you try, do try this one – I promise you, it's heaven.
And if you've fallen out with your partner, make these and you'll kiss and make up in no time!*

1 quantity Croissant dough (*see* page 48)
3 Terry's Chocolate Oranges
1 egg, beaten, for eggwash
Apricot jam, warmed, to glaze

MAKES 24 PAINS AU CHOCOLAT

Make the croissant dough as on page 48 up to the point where it is ready to shape.

Line several baking trays. Cut the dough in half and roll out each piece into a
40cm/16 inch square. Cut into 12 x 10cm/5 x 4 inch rectangles. Put two segments
of Chocolate Orange at the short end of each rectangle and roll up into a parcel.
Pinch the ends together to seal. Place on the baking trays, then brush each one with
the eggwash and leave to rise for 1 hour.

Preheat the oven to 200°C/400°F/gas mark 6. Bake for 15 minutes until golden
brown, then remove from the oven and brush each one with warm apricot jam.

ITALIAN BREADS

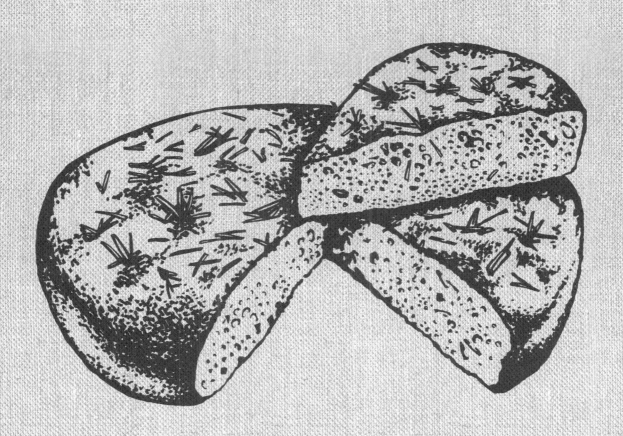

CIABATTA

This recipe is perfect for making pizzas and garlic bread: simply flatten the dough out and use as a pizza base or brush with garlic oil and you have instant garlic bread.

500g (1lb 2oz) strong white flour, plus extra for dusting
325ml (11fl oz) water
30g (1oz) yeast
10g (⅓oz) salt
30ml (1fl oz) olive oil

MAKES 4 LOAVES

Put 300g (10½oz) of the flour into a bowl with the water and yeast. Using a hand whisk, whisk for 5 minutes, then leave to ferment for 4 hours.

Add the remaining flour and water, the salt and olive oil. Whisk briskly for 5 minutes, then leave in the bowl for 2 hours.

Tip the dough out onto a lightly floured surface and divide it into two equal pieces. Stretch each piece of dough into a 20.5cm/8 inch loaf, then allow to rest for 1 hour.

Line two baking trays. Divide each piece of dough into two. Stretch each of the four loaves back to 20.5cm/8 inches, transfer to the baking trays and leave to rest for 1 hour.

Preheat the oven to 200°C/400°F/gas mark 6. Dust the loaves with flour and bake for 20 minutes until golden brown, then transfer to a wire rack to cool.

HAM & CREAM PIZZA

The idea for this pizza came from a Sicilian friend who had moved to Cyprus, opened a pizzeria and built a beehive oven to bake the pizzas in. The secret of a good pizza is to use fresh ingredients and to keep the flavours simple – you want to be able to taste the ciabatta base and not have it overwhelmed by the toppings.

FOR THE TOMATO SAUCE
2 tablespoons olive oil
1 small onion, peeled and finely chopped
1 garlic clove, peeled and chopped
1 tablespoon tomato purée
400g (14oz) can chopped tomatoes
2 tablespoons freshly chopped basil
2 bay leaves
1 teaspoon caster sugar
Salt and freshly ground black pepper

FOR THE PIZZA
1 quantity Ciabatta dough (*see* page 54)
Flour, for dusting
60g (2¼oz) Gorgonzola blue cheese, crumbled
150g (5½oz) mozzarella cheese, crumbled
175g (6oz) mature Cheddar cheese, crumbled
7 tablespooons double cream
8 thin slices of Virginia ham

MAKES 1 LARGE PIZZA

To make the sauce, heat the oil in a pan and sauté the onion until translucent, then add the garlic and fry gently for a further minute. Stir in the rest of the ingredients and season to taste. Bring the sauce to the boil, then simmer for about 30 minutes. Before using, remove the bay leaves.

Meanwhile, preheat the oven to 230°C/450°F/gas mark 8. Roll out the dough on a lightly floured surface to a 32cm/12½ inch diameter circle and place on a large baking tray. Bake for 5 minutes (this kills the yeast in the dough).

Lightly spread the tomato sauce onto the pizza base and sprinkle with the Gorgonzola, then cover with the mozzarella and Cheddar cheeses. Pour the double cream all over the pizza and bake for 20–25 minutes until golden brown.

Take the pizza out of the oven and place thin layers of ham on top. Serve immediately.

TOMATO BRUSCHETTA

Bruschetta is great party food and you can make it just a couple of hours before your guests arrive. It also makes a good snack.

450g (1lb) ripe tomatoes, peeled
  and cut into small pieces
3 tablespoons olive oil
10 basil leaves, torn
Salt and freshly ground black pepper, to taste
8 ciabatta slices (*see* page 54)
2 garlic cloves, peeled and halved

SERVES 4

Put the tomatoes in the oil with the basil leaves, season to taste and leave to marinate.

Toast the ciabatta, then rub each side with the garlic. Spoon some of the tomato mixture onto each slice and serve warm.

OLIVE BRUSCHETTA

200g (7oz) black olives, pitted
Juice of 1 lemon
1 tablespoon olive oil
Salt and freshly ground black pepper, to taste
8 ciabatta slices (*see* page 54)
2 garlic cloves, peeled and halved

SERVES 4

Put the olives, lemon juice and oil in a mixer and whiz for 2 minutes to a smooth paste. Season to taste.

Toast the ciabatta, then rub each side with the garlic. Cover each slice with the olive mixture and serve warm.

BASIL & OLIVE FOCACCIA

The aromas in your kitchen when making this are unbelievable. If you're trying to sell your house make this an hour before the potential buyers view it. A sale is guaranteed.

500g (1lb 2oz) strong white flour, plus extra for dusting
5g (⅛oz) salt
100ml (3½fl oz) olive oil
20g (¾oz) yeast
300ml (½ pint) water
125g (4½oz) black olives, pitted but left whole
Handful of freshly chopped basil leaves
Salt water made with 15g (½oz) salt dissolved in 60ml (2fl oz) warm water

MAKES 1 LOAF

Put the flour, salt, half the olive oil, the yeast and water into a large bowl and mix with your hand for 3 minutes until all the flour has been picked up.

Tip the dough out onto a lightly floured surface and knead well for 6 minutes. The dough should be quite sticky. Put the dough back in the bowl and leave at room temperature for 2 hours.

Line a baking tray. Mix 100g (3½oz) of the olives and all the basil into the dough, then flatten the dough out onto the baking tray to a circle about 20cm/8 inches in diameter. Brush the top of the dough with a little olive oil and make indentations in the top with your fingers. Leave to rise for 1 hour.

Preheat the oven to 230°C/450°F/gas mark 8. Brush the top of the dough with the salt water and drizzle with the remaining olive oil, then stud the remaining olives into the dough.

Bake for 20–25 minutes until golden brown, then transfer to a wire rack to cool a little. Serve warm with an olive salad.

FOCACCIA PUGLIESE WITH MOZZARELLA

This is based on a bread I made while working in Italy in 2002. You do not need the sun belting down — but it helps!

500g (1lb 2oz) strong white flour, plus extra for dusting
10g (⅓oz) salt
20g (¾oz) yeast
100ml (3½fl oz) olive oil
300ml (½ pint) water
Salt water made from 15g (½oz) salt dissolved in 60ml (2fl oz) warm water
2 balls of buffalo mozzarella, drained and torn into pieces

MAKES 2 SMALL LOAVES

Put the flour, salt, yeast, half the olive oil and all the water into a bowl and mix together to make a pliable dough. Tip the dough out onto a lightly floured surface and knead for 5 minutes. Put the dough back in the bowl and leave to rest for 1 hour.

Line a baking tray. Divide the dough into two equal pieces. Stretch the dough out with your hands so it is about 2cm/¾ inch thick and oval in shape. Put it on the baking tray and prick the top with a knife (this will restrict its growth). Brush the top with the salt water and the remaining olive oil. Cover the top of the bread with the mozzarella, then leave the dough to rise for 45 minutes.

Preheat the oven to 220°C/425°F/gas mark 7. Bake for 25 minutes, then transfer to a wire rack to cool. Serve with an olive salad and a glass of good Tuscan wine like Montepulciano.

FOCACCIA PUGLIESE
WITH TOMATOES & GARLIC

Focaccia is both gorgeous to look at and to eat. It epitomizes the Italian philosophy on bread – simple but effective flavourings. You will need to prepare the garlic oil the night before.

4 garlic cloves, peeled and crushed
125ml (4fl oz) olive oil
500g (1lb 2oz) strong white flour, plus extra for dusting
10g (⅓oz) salt
20g (¾oz) yeast
250ml (9fl oz) water
Salt water made from 15g (½oz) salt dissolved in 60ml (2fl oz) warm water
2–3 plum tomatoes, thinly sliced

MAKES 1 LOAF

Add the garlic to the olive oil, then leave to infuse overnight.

Put the flour, salt, yeast, 75ml (2½fl oz) of the infused olive oil and all the water into a large bowl and mix together for 4 minutes. Tip out onto a lightly floured surface and knead for 6 minutes, then put back in the bowl to rest for 1 hour.

Line a baking tray. Tip the dough out onto a floured surface and roll out a rectangle measuring about 28 x 22cm/11 x 8½ inches. Place on the baking tray and sprinkle with the salt water and the remaining olive oil. Then, using a knife, prick the top of the dough all over. Place the tomatoes on top of the dough and leave to rise for 1 hour.

Preheat the oven to 220°C/425°F/gas mark 7. Bake for 20–25 minutes until golden brown. Serve warm.

POTATO FOCACCIA PUGLIESE

I made this with a couple of Sicilian friends when I was in Italy, and was astounded by the flavours from the potatoes – they marry so well with the rosemary and bread.

500g (1lb 2oz) strong white flour, plus extra for dusting
5g (⅛oz) salt
20g (¾oz) yeast
300ml (½ pint) water
4–5 new potatoes, scrubbed and thinly sliced
Olive oil
Rock salt
2 sprigs of fresh rosemary, destalked

MAKES 1 LOAF

Put the flour, salt, yeast and water into a bowl and mix to form a dough. Leave in the bowl to double in size for about 1 hour.

Cook the potatoes in boiling, salted water for 2 minutes to soften. Drain.

Line a baking tray. Tip the dough out onto the baking tray and flatten with your hands, then brush with olive oil and, using your fingers, make indentations over the surface. Layer the potatoes over the top, sprinkle with a little rock salt and stud with the rosemary sprigs. Leave to rise on the baking tray for 1 hour.

Preheat the oven to 230°C/450°F/gas mark 8. Bake for 25 minutes until golden. Remove from the oven and brush the loaf with more olive oil, then transfer to a wire rack and serve when cooled.

MUSHROOM & ONION FOCACCIA

This focaccia perfectly complements tomato-based pasta dishes and thick winter soups. For extra richness, drizzle over a little olive oil and sprinkle with chopped garlic.

15g (½oz) dried porcini mushrooms
60ml (2fl oz) olive oil, plus extra for frying and drizzling
100g (3½oz) button mushrooms, roughly chopped
2 red onions, peeled
500g (1lb 2oz) strong white flour
10g (⅓oz) salt
15g (½oz) yeast
Rock salt

MAKES 2 LOAVES

Put the dried porcini mushrooms in a bowl. Add 150ml (¼ pint) boiling water and leave to soak for 20 minutes. Drain, reserving the liquid. Heat a drizzle of oil in a frying pan and fry the button mushrooms for 4–5 minutes until lightly browned. Finely chop the fresh and dried mushrooms by hand or in a food processor. Make the reserved liquid up to 225ml (8fl oz) with water. Finely chop one of the onions.

Put the flour, salt, yeast and olive oil into a bowl. Add the mushroom water, chopped mushrooms and onion to make a dough, adding a dash more water if the dough feels dry. Tip the dough out onto a lightly floured surface and knead well for 5 minutes. When the dough is pliable, put back in the bowl, cover and leave to rest for about 1 hour.

Roughly chop the remaining onion and fry in a little more oil until deep golden.

Line a baking tray. Divide the dough in half and flatten each half out on the baking tray to an oval about 26cm/10½ inches long.

Using your fingers, make indentations all over the dough, brush lightly with olive oil and sprinkle with rock salt. Scatter with the fried onion, then leave to prove for 1 hour.

Preheat the oven to 200°C/400°F/gas mark 6. Bake for 20–30 minutes until golden brown. Serve warm.

OLIVE & SUN-DRIED TOMATO BREAD

You can use sunblushed tomatoes in this recipe – they work just as well. The aromas in your kitchen while you are making this bread will tempt not just you, but your neighbours, too.

500g (1lb 2oz) strong white flour, plus extra for dusting
5g (⅛oz) salt
40ml (1½fl oz) olive oil
20g (¾oz) yeast
300ml (½ pint) warm water
150g (5½oz) black Greek olives, pitted and roughly chopped
100g (3½oz) sun-dried tomatoes, chopped

MAKES 2 LOAVES

Put the flour in a large bowl and add the salt, olive oil and yeast. Slowly add the warm water, folding it in with your hand until the dough becomes pliable.

Tip the dough out onto a lightly floured surface and knead for 5 minutes, then return the dough to the bowl, cover and leave for 1 hour in a warm place.

Line a baking tray. Add the olives and tomatoes to the dough and work in well. Divide the dough into two equal pieces. Mould each into a round shape and press down firmly to flatten. Put on the baking tray, sprinkle with a little flour and mark a cross in each. Leave to prove for 1 hour in a warm place.

Preheat the oven to 220°C/425°F/gas mark 7. Bake for about 25–30 minutes until golden brown, then transfer to a wire rack to cool.

TOMATO & BASIL BREAD

This is an Italian-inspired bread from Tuscany. Their tomatoes are so juicy and full of flavour that it was a natural thing to try them out in one of my breads.

Try drying the tomatoes yourself in an oven – cut them into slices, drizzle with olive oil and leave in a low oven – 110°C/225°F/gas mark ¼ – overnight.

500g (1lb 2oz) strong white flour, plus extra for dusting
10g (⅓oz) salt
20g (¾oz) yeast
60ml (2fl oz) olive oil
275ml (9½fl oz) water
100g (3½oz) sunblushed tomatoes, roughly chopped
30g (1oz) fresh basil, roughly chopped

MAKES 1 LOAF

Put the flour, salt, yeast, oil and water into a bowl and mix gently by hand to bring them together. When all the flour has been incorporated, tip the dough out onto a lightly floured surface and knead for 5 minutes. When the dough is pliable, transfer it to the bowl, cover and leave to rest for about 1 hour.

Line a baking tray. Add the tomatoes and basil to the dough and work in well. Stretch and squeeze the dough into a sausage at least 70cm/28 inches long and tie in a knot. Place on the baking tray and leave to rise for 1 hour.

Preheat the oven to 230°C/450°F/gas mark 8. Bake for 30 minutes until golden brown, then transfer to a wire rack to cool.

PANE TOSCANO

You need to start this the day before. The lack of salt in the recipe will be compensated for by the fermentation of the dough.

500g (1lb 2oz) Italian tipo 00 flour,
  plus extra for dusting
15g (½oz) yeast
250ml (9fl oz) water
60ml (2fl oz) olive oil

MAKES 1 LOAF

Put half the flour and all the yeast and water into a bowl, and mix until you have a thick batter. Leave to rise for 9 hours or overnight.

Mix in the remaining flour and the olive oil and knead for 5 minutes. Leave in the bowl to rise for 1 hour.

Line a baking tray. Tip the dough out onto a lightly floured surface and shape into a ball. Rub flour all over the ball so it is covered, then make several slashes randomly all over the loaf. Leave to rise on the baking tray for 1 hour.

Preheat the oven to 220°C/425°F/gas mark 7. Bake for 30 minutes, then leave to cool slightly and serve warm.

PANE TOSCANO WITH DOLCELATTE

I spent the summer of 2002 in and around Tuscany making bread with local bakers. This bread brings back good memories. You need to start this the day before.

500g (1lb 2oz) Italian tipo 00 flour,
  plus extra for dusting
15g (½oz) yeast
250ml (9fl oz) water
60ml (2fl oz) olive oil
150g (5½oz) dolcelatte cheese

MAKES 1 LOAF

Put half the flour and all the yeast and water into a bowl, and mix until you have a thick batter. Leave to rise for 9 hours.

Line a baking tray. Add the remaining flour and the olive oil to the dough and mix in well, then knead for 5 minutes. Gradually add the cheese – it will get very messy but persevere, and add a little flour if it gets too wet. Leave in the bowl to rise for 1 hour.

Tip the dough out onto a lightly floured surface. Roll up into a sausage about 60cm/23½ inches long and join the ends together. Put on the baking tray, dust with flour and leave to rise for 1 hour.

Preheat the oven to 220°C/425°F/gas mark 7. Bake for 30 minutes, allow to cool a little and serve warm.

GRISSINI STICKS

These make great snack food; my son Joshua loves them. They can be frozen in dough form and thawed in about 3 hours.

250g (9oz) strong white flour,
  plus extra for dusting
½ teaspoon salt
5g (⅛oz) yeast
2 tablespoons olive oil
150ml (¼ pint) water
Sesame or poppy seeds

MAKES ABOUT 22–25 STICKS

Put the flour, salt, yeast and olive oil into a bowl and mix together. Gradually add the water and mix until all the flour has been incorporated from the sides of the bowl. Tip the dough out onto a lightly floured surface and knead for 5 minutes. Return the dough to the bowl and leave to rest for 30 minutes.

Preheat the oven to 220°C/425°F/gas mark 7. Line two baking trays. Rip the dough into 15–20g (½–¾oz) pieces and, without using any flour, roll each out under the palm of your hands into thin strips about 25.5cm/10 inches in length. Moisten your hands a little and roll each strip in sesame or poppy seeds, then place on the baking trays. Bake for 20 minutes until golden brown.

CHEESE STRAWS

This is a recipe that is used in several well-known hotels. The straws are very quick to make and when the pastry is baked it doubles in size and is a real mouthful.

500g (1lb 2oz) packet ready-made puff pastry
Flour, for dusting
1 egg, beaten
10g (⅓oz) paprika
200g (7oz) Parmesan cheese, finely grated

MAKES 30–40 STICKS

Roll out the puff pastry on a lightly floured surface to a 50 x 25cm/20 x 10 inch rectangle and brush with beaten egg. Sprinkle with the paprika and coat generously with the Parmesan, pressing down gently.

Fold one-third of the pastry up over the filling and the remaining third down to create three layers. Rest the pastry in the fridge for 30 minutes. Repeat this twice more.

Preheat the oven to 200°C/400°F/gas mark 6. Line several baking trays. Roll out the dough to 5mm/¼ inch thick and cut into long, thin strips. Twist each strip in opposite directions to create a spiral effect, then place on the baking trays and bake for 10–15 minutes until golden. Serve warm.

TRADITIONAL BREADS

NAAN BREAD

Authentic naan needs to be baked in a specially made brick oven, but I decided to shallow-fry the dough instead, which gives it this light and fluffy, golden finish. It's excellent as finger food, cut into thin slices and served with a chilled aubergine and crème fraîche dip.

500g (1lb 2oz) strong white flour,
  plus extra for dusting
10g (⅓oz) salt
15g (½oz) yeast
1 teaspoon cumin seeds
1 teaspoon caraway seeds
325ml (11fl oz) water
Olive oil, for frying

MAKES 3 NAANS

Line a baking tray. Put the flour, salt, yeast and seeds into a bowl and add enough water to make a soft, but not sloppy dough. Divide the dough into three pieces, put on the baking tray and leave to rest for 1 hour.

Turn the dough out onto a lightly floured surface and, using a rolling pin, flatten each piece into a circle 25.5cm/10 inches in diameter. Leave to rest for 5 minutes.

Heat a frying pan to a medium heat and add a splash of olive oil. Shallow-fry each naan until browned on both sides, then set aside to cool slightly before serving.

CURRIED NAAN BREAD

I was asked by a chef to come up with a naan to go with his extensive buffet. I love curries, so this was the obvious recipe. ILLUSTRATED

500g (1lb 2oz) strong white flour,
  plus extra for dusting
10g (⅓oz) salt
1 tablespoon olive oil, plus extra for frying
50g (1¾oz) mild curry powder
15g (½oz) yeast
300ml (½ pint) water
100g (3½oz) sultanas
3 tablespoons mango chutney

MAKES 6 NAANS

Put the flour, salt, oil, curry powder, yeast and water into a bowl and mix together for 2 minutes. Tip out onto a lightly floured surface and knead for 5 minutes until the dough is soft and pliable. Leave to rise for 30 minutes.

Line a baking tray. Incorporate the sultanas and chutney into the dough. Divide the dough into six equal pieces, put on the baking tray and leave to rest for 1 hour.

Turn the dough out onto a lightly floured surface and, using a rolling pin, roll each piece into a circle 25.5cm/10 inches in diameter. Leave to rest for 5 minutes.

Heat a frying pan to a medium heat and add a splash of olive oil. Shallow-fry each naan until browned on both sides, then set aside to cool slightly before serving.

SPICED PARATHA WITH SULTANAS

Paratha is a very moist, chewy bread – great for dunking in curry. It can be fried in a frying pan.

400g (14oz) wholemeal flour, plus extra for dusting
3 tablespoons vegetable oil, plus extra for frying
1 teaspoon salt
225ml (8fl oz) water

FOR THE FILLING
1 tablespoon vegetable oil
1 teaspoon cumin seeds
2 green chillies, deseeded and finely chopped
2 teaspoons ground coriander
30g (1oz) sultanas

MAKES 12 PARATHAS

Put the flour, oil and salt into a large bowl and slowly mix in the water to form a dough. Knead until smooth, then cover the dough with a clean cloth and leave for 20 minutes.

Meanwhile, make the filling. Heat the oil in a frying pan and add the cumin seeds and chillies. Fry, stirring, for 1 minute, then add the ground coriander and sultanas and mix well. Cook gently, stirring now and then, for 2 minutes, then put to one side.

Divide the dough into 12 small balls and lightly coat each ball with flour. Roll out onto a lightly floured surface to form thin, round, flat breads, or parathas, about 15cm/6 inches in diameter. Sprinkle the filling over half of each round and fold the other half over. Flatten with a rolling pin to secure the filling in place.

Heat a griddle pan until hot. Brush one side of a paratha with a little oil and place on the griddle, oiled-side down. Brush the top with more oil. Once the paratha has cooked underneath, after about 3 minutes, turn it over and cook the other side until golden brown.

Repeat the process with the remaining parathas. Serve warm.

LAVROCHE

This recipe haunted me for many a year while I was living in Cyprus – making 500 of these a day was not my idea of fun. But this is a great recipe, given to me by George Demitriades, ex-pastry chef at the Annabelle Hotel, Paphos.

The breads make a great pre-dinner nibble, served with drinks, or they can be eaten with cheese at the end of the meal.

250g (9oz) strong white flour, plus extra for dusting
100g (3½oz) semolina
5g (⅛oz) salt
1 tablespoon olive oil
100ml (3½fl oz) water
75ml (2½fl oz) milk
1 egg, beaten, for eggwash
100g (3½oz) sesame seeds

FILLS 3 BAKING TRAYS

Put all the ingredients, except the eggwash and sesame seeds, into a bowl and mix well, then, using your hands, knead for 5 minutes until you have a pliable dough. Cover and leave to stand for 20 minutes.

Preheat the oven to 220°C/425°F/gas mark 7. Line three baking trays. Tip the dough out onto a lightly floured surface and, using a rolling pin, roll out until it is wafer thin – about 2–3mm/⅛ inch thick. Use plenty of flour, but brush it off afterwards.

Brush with the eggwash and cover the top with the sesame seeds. Cut the dough into random shapes and place on the baking trays. Bake for 15–20 minutes until dark brown, then serve immediately.

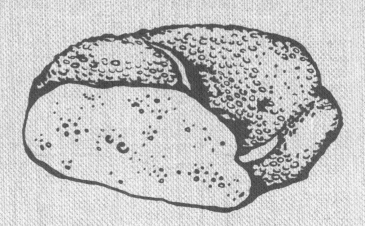

CYPRIOT OLIVE & CORIANDER BREAD

This recipe comes from a tiny village called Kouklia, in the south of Cyprus. Bread making is a social occasion for Cypriots and I spent one marvellous afternoon with friends making bread for the whole village. Afterwards we sat and ate the warm loaves with hummus, tzatziki, grilled meats and salad – fantastic!

500g (1lb 2oz) strong white flour, plus extra for dusting
5g (⅛oz) salt
30ml (1fl oz) olive oil
20g (¾oz) yeast
300ml (½ pint) warm water
150g (5½oz) black Greek olives, pitted and chopped
75g (3oz) onion, peeled and chopped
Handful of fresh coriander leaves, chopped

MAKES 2 LOAVES

Put the flour into a large bowl and add the salt and oil. Dilute the yeast in a little warm water and add to the mixture. Slowly add the warm water, folding it in with your hand until the dough becomes pliable.

Tip the dough out onto a lightly floured surface and knead for 5 minutes, then put the dough back in the bowl, cover and leave for 1 hour in a warm place.

Line a baking tray. Work the olives, onion and coriander into the dough, and cut in half. Mould each piece into a round shape, put on the baking tray and press down firmly. Sprinkle lightly with flour and mark a cross in each, then leave in a warm place for 1 hour.

Preheat the oven to 220°C/425°F/gas mark 7. Bake for 25–30 minutes until golden brown, then transfer to a wire rack to cool.

KOULOURI
CYPRIOT VILLAGE BREAD

When I lived in Cyprus, every Sunday I would visit the villages of my friends and invariably make bread. This bread is very common in Cyprus and is best served with dips and a good olive salad. Gum mastic and mahlab are used in many Greek/Cypriot dishes. They have a similar flavour to fennel or aniseed, the seeds of which you can use as substitutes. However, they should be available from specialist delicatessens or online.

Pinch of gum mastic powder
Pinch of mahlab powder
500g (1lb 2oz) strong white flour, plus extra for dusting
5g (⅛oz) salt
20g (¾oz) yeast
60ml (2fl oz) olive oil
250ml (9fl oz) water
40g (1½oz) sesame seeds
½ teaspoon black cumin seeds
½ teaspoon caraway seeds

MAKES 1 LOAF

Put the flour, salt, yeast, olive oil and water in a large bowl and blend together. Add the gum mastic and mahlab powders and knead for 5 minutes, then leave the dough in the bowl to rest for 1 hour.

Tip the sesame, black cumin and caraway seeds into a large bowl and cover with warm water. This will balloon the seeds and release their flavours. Drain thoroughly and scatter on a sheet of parchment paper.

Line a baking tray. Tip the dough out onto a lightly floured surface and shape into a ball. Drop the dough into the dampened seeds and turn until covered in the seeds, then place the dough on the baking tray and leave to rise for 1 hour.

Preheat the oven to 220°C/425°F/gas mark 7. Using a knife, make a cut around the middle of the ball and two on top. Bake for 30 minutes until golden brown, then transfer to a wire rack to cool.

HALOUMI & MINT BREAD

This is a traditional Cypriot bread and is eaten throughout the year in Cyprus.

500g (1lb 2oz) strong white flour, plus extra for dusting
½ teaspoon salt
1–2 teaspoons dried mint
60ml (2fl oz) olive oil
20g (¾oz) yeast
265ml (9½fl oz) water
250g (9oz) haloumi cheese, crumbled

MAKES I LOAF

Put the flour, salt, mint, olive oil and yeast into a bowl and add the water to bring the ingredients together. Mix for 3 minutes, then tip out onto a lightly floured surface and knead for 5 minutes. (If you are using a food mixer, use the hook and mix for 5 minutes in total.) Put the dough back in the bowl and leave to rise for 1 hour.

Line a baking tray. Add the cheese to the dough and shape into a sausage. Taper the ends and place on the baking tray to rest for 1 hour.

Preheat the oven to 220°C/425°F/gas mark 7. Cut diagonal slashes across the top of the dough and dust with flour. Bake for 35–40 minutes until golden brown, then transfer to a wire rack to cool.

LAGANES BREAD

A traditional bread made in Cyprus around Green Monday, the day the fasting starts before Easter. The bread is usually eaten with fresh vegetables and fruit.

Try using ground fennel if gum mastic powder is difficult to get hold of, but specialist delicatessens should stock it.

1 teaspoon gum mastic powder
500g (1lb 2oz) strong white flour, plus extra for dusting
10g (⅓oz) salt
20g (¾oz) yeast
60ml (2fl oz) olive oil
275ml (9½fl oz) water
75g (3oz) sesame seeds
1 tablespoon caraway seeds
1½ tablespoons black cumin seeds

MAKES 2 LOAVES

Put the flour, salt, yeast, olive oil and water into a bowl and mix together for 3 minutes. Add the gum mastic powder to the dough, then tip the dough out onto a lightly floured surface. Using your fingers and the heel of your palm, knead for 5 minutes, then put the dough back in the bowl and leave to rise for 1 hour.

Meanwhile, put the sesame, caraway and black cumin seeds into a bowl and pour over just enough warm water to cover. Leave for 20 minutes – this balloons the seeds and releases their flavours. Drain thoroughly and tip out onto a sheet of parchment paper.

Line a baking tray. Tip the dough out onto a floured surface and divide into two equal pieces. Flatten each piece into an oval shape 1.5cm/¾ inch thick. Turn them in the seed mixture, pressing the seeds firmly into the dough until completely covered, top and bottom. Put on the baking tray and leave to rise for 1 hour.

Preheat the oven to 220°C/425°F/gas mark 7. Using a finger, press holes over the top of the dough. Bake for 20 minutes until golden brown. Transfer to a wire rack to cool.

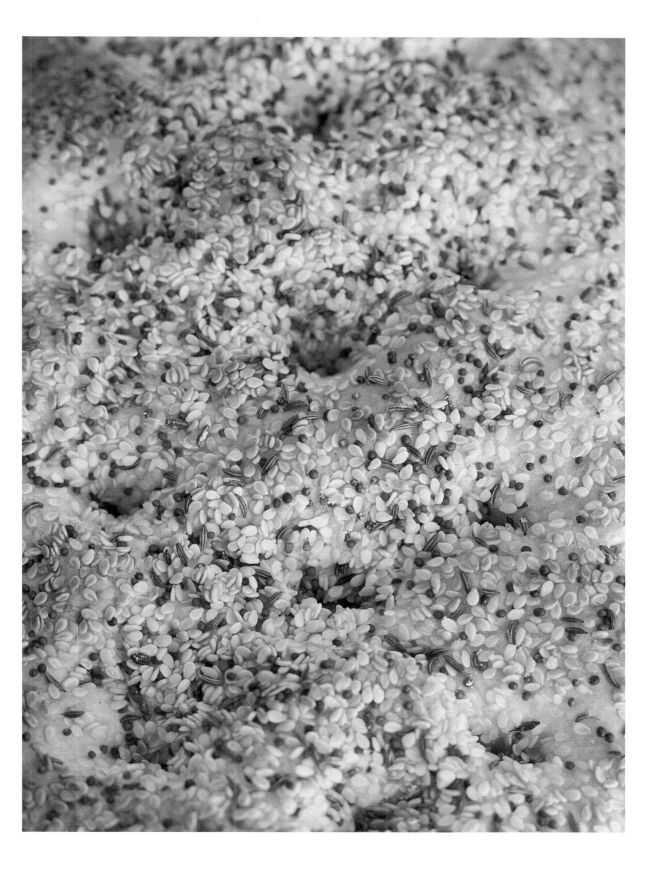

TSOUREKI
CYPRIOT EASTER BREAD

I have kept this bread as authentic as possible. You will find the gum mastic and mahlab powders in specialist delicatessens, but you can use ground fennel and ground anise as alternatives. I've made this bread several times on TV and it remains a firm favourite.

500g (1lb 2oz) strong white flour, plus extra for dusting
60g (2¼oz) butter, softened
75g (3oz) caster sugar
Pinch of ground cinnamon
Pinch of gum mastic powder
Pinch of mahlab powder
Handful of sultanas
150ml (¼ pint) milk
Zest of 1 orange
10g (⅓oz) salt
15g (½oz) yeast
150ml (¼ pint) warm water
3 eggs, hard-boiled in their shells with red food colouring
1 egg, beaten, for eggwash

MAKES I LOAF

Put the flour into a large bowl with all the other ingredients except the yeast, water and eggs, and mix together briefly. Dilute the yeast in the warm water and add to the mixture. Mix until you have a soft dough.

Tip the dough out onto a lightly floured surface and knead until you have a pliable dough. Put the dough back in the bowl and leave to rest for 1 hour.

Line a baking tray. Divide the dough into two equal pieces and roll into two 55cm/ 22 inch strips. Plait the strips together, put on the baking tray and leave to rise in a warm place for 1 hour.

Preheat the oven to 200°C/400°F/gas mark 6. Brush the top of the bread with the eggwash and nestle the coloured eggs along the top of the bread. Bake for 25 minutes, then transfer to a wire rack to cool.

KULICH

A traditional bread made in Eastern Europe and shaped like one of the domes that top a Russian Orthodox church. It makes a great afternoon treat.

FOR THE BREAD
500g (1lb 2oz) strong white flour, plus extra for dusting
5g (⅛oz) salt
75g (3oz) caster sugar
75g (3oz) butter, softened
30g (1oz) fresh yeast
2 teaspoons vanilla extract
Zest of 2 oranges
Zest of 2 lemons
2 medium eggs
175ml (6fl oz) milk
100g (3½oz) sultanas
75g (3oz) flaked almonds

FOR THE ICING
65g (2½oz) icing sugar
1 tablespoon lemon juice

MAKES 2 LOAVES

Put the flour, salt, sugar, butter, yeast, vanilla extract, the orange and lemon zests and eggs into a bowl and blend with a little milk just to bring the ingredients together. Slowly add the rest of the milk, mixing with your hands, until you have a soft dough.

Tip the dough out onto a lightly floured surface and knead for a few minutes. Put the dough back in the bowl and leave to rise for 1 hour.

Line two clean flowerpots or tins with silicone paper. Incorporate the sultanas and almonds into the dough, then divide the dough into two and shape each piece so that it fits into the flowerpots or tins. Leave to rise for 1 hour.

Preheat the oven to 200°C/400°F/gas mark 6. Bake the flowerpots or tins in the oven for 30–40 minutes until golden brown, then turn out onto a wire rack to cool.

While it is cooling, make the icing. Tip the icing sugar into a bowl, then add the lemon juice and mix in well, adding some water if necessary, until the icing coats the back of a spoon. Top the bread with the icing and serve.

PESACH (PASSOVER) BREAD

This recipe was given to me by Sylvia Woolf when I appeared on the This Morning show. It has a great texture and flavour.

250g (9oz) medium matzo meal
1 teaspoon salt
1 teaspoon caster sugar
240ml (8fl oz) water
120ml (4fl oz) oil
4 medium eggs

MAKES I LOAF

Put the matzo meal, salt and sugar into a bowl and mix well.

Put the water and oil in a large saucepan and bring to the boil. Remove from the heat, add the meal mixture and stir until the dough comes away from the sides. Leave to cool for 5 minutes.

Add the eggs, one at a time, and stir until the mixture is smooth and thick.

Line a baking tray. Flatten the dough out to 1cm/½ inch thickness on the baking tray and prick all over with a fork. Leave it to rest for 30 minutes.

Preheat the oven to 190°C/375°F/gas mark 5. Bake for 25–30 minutes until browned.

PITTA BREAD

A traditional Arabic bread that has been made for over 3,000 years. Originally it was made with a sour culture in place of yeast and baked on olive domes set over fires.

500g (1lb 2oz) strong white flour,
  plus extra for dusting
10g (⅓oz) salt
50g (1¾oz) caster sugar
60ml (2fl oz) olive oil
30g (1oz) yeast
300ml (½ pint) water

MAKES 9 PITTAS

Put all the ingredients into a bowl and mix with your hands to bind together to a dough. Tip out onto a lightly floured surface and knead for 5 minutes. Put back in the bowl and rest the dough for 1 hour.

Preheat the oven to 240°C/475°F/gas mark 9 and put a baking tray inside to heat up. Tip the dough out onto the table and divide it into nine 100g (3½oz) pieces. Using a rolling pin, roll out the dough into 20cm/8 inch ovals. Leave to rest on the table for 5 minutes, then place on the hot baking tray and bake for 5–10 minutes. The bread will balloon, but when you bring the pittas out of the oven they will collapse, forming the characteristic pockets of air.

PEPPER & ONION FLOWERPOT BREAD

The Ancient Egyptians used to bake their bread in cone-shaped terracotta pots and this is the contemporary version, although the herbs and onions are authentic ingredients. This bread is particularly good for dinner parties – the little pots are very eye-catching and you could even try painting them for extra effect.

10g (⅓oz) salt
50g (1¾oz) butter, softened
500g (1lb 2oz) strong white flour
20g (¾oz) yeast
300ml (½ pint) warm water
1 large onion, peeled and finely chopped
Olive oil, for frying
2 red peppers, deseeded and finely chopped
30g (1oz) fresh basil, roughly chopped

MAKES 3 LOAVES

You will need three flowerpots for this recipe, each 10cm/4 inches in diameter and 25.5cm/10 inches high.

Add the salt and butter to the flour and rub together. Dilute the yeast in a little water and add this to the flour, then mix in enough warm water to make the dough pliable. Knead the dough well for 5 minutes, until elasticated. Place in a bowl, cover and leave in a warm place to rest for 1 hour.

Fry the onion in a little olive oil until translucent, then set aside to cool. Pat the peppers dry on kitchen paper. When cool, mix the onion with the peppers and basil, add to the dough and blend together. Divide the dough into three equal pieces and shape them into balls.

Line the sides and base of the flowerpots with silicone paper. Place a ball of dough inside each pot and leave to prove for 1 hour.

Preheat the oven to 200°C/400°F/gas mark 6. Bake the flowerpots for 20–25 minutes. Turn the breads out onto a wire rack to cool, then return them to the unlined flowerpots for display on your dining table.

HERB & SEED
BREADS

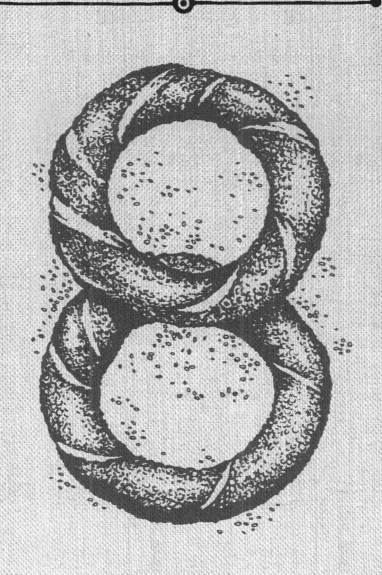

HERB BREAD

This is an aromatic bread, full of flavour. Basil is a favourite herb of mine, and mixed with coriander it's perfect. This bread is great as a base for cheese on toast.

500g (1lb 2oz) strong white flour, plus extra for dusting
10g (⅓oz) salt
20g (¾oz) yeast
75ml (2½fl oz) olive oil
250ml (9fl oz) water
20g (¾oz) fresh basil, roughly chopped
20g (¾oz) fresh coriander, roughly chopped
20g (¾oz) fresh dill, roughly chopped

MAKES 2 LOAVES

Put the flour, salt, yeast, olive oil and water into a bowl and, using your hands, mix together for 3 minutes. When the dough has formed, tip out onto a lightly floured surface and, using your fingers and heel of your palm, knead for 3 minutes. Add the herbs and knead for a further 3 minutes. Put the dough back in the bowl and leave to rise for 1 hour.

Preheat the oven to 220°C/425°F/gas mark 7. Line a baking tray. Divide the dough into two equal pieces and shape each into a ball. Flatten slightly with your hands and place on the baking tray. Cut two slashes across the top of each and leave to rise for 1 hour, then bake for 25 minutes. Transfer to a wire rack to cool.

RICOTTA & CHIVE LOAF

You can also try making this recipe with Philadelphia cream cheese instead of ricotta, for a creamy bread with tight airholes. Either way, served toasted with cheese it is unbeatable.

500g (1lb 2oz) strong white flour, plus extra for dusting
10g (⅓oz) salt
20g (¾oz) yeast
75ml (2½fl oz) olive oil
250ml (9fl oz) water
125g (4½oz) ricotta cheese
4 tablespoons snipped chives

MAKES 1 LOAF

Put the flour, salt, yeast, olive oil, water and cheese into a large bowl and mix with your hands for 3 minutes. Tip out onto a lightly floured surface and knead for 2 minutes, then add the chives and knead for a futher 3 minutes. Put the dough back in the bowl and leave to rest for 1 hour.

Line a baking tray. Tip the dough out onto a lightly floured surface and shape into a sausage, tapered at each end. Place the bread on the baking tray and leave to rise for 1 hour.

Preheat the oven to 220°C/425°F/gas mark 7. Bake for 30 minutes, then transfer to a wire rack to cool.

POTATO & DILL BREAD

This bread is definitely a meal on its own – serve it as a sandwich, thinly sliced, filled with roast garlic lamb and salad leaves with a lemon dressing. Topped with cheese, it also makes a great accompaniment to a thick soup. You need to start this bread the day before.

20g (¾oz) yeast
300ml (½ pint) warm water
500g (1lb 2oz) strong white flour, plus extra for dusting
10g (⅓oz) salt
400g (14oz) new potatoes, scrubbed
Butter and olive oil, for frying
1 garlic clove, peeled and chopped
30g (1oz) fresh dill, destalked and chopped

MAKES 2 LOAVES

Dilute the yeast in a little warm water. Put the flour and salt into a bowl, and add the diluted yeast. Slowly add enough water to the flour until you have a malleable dough, then leave to rest overnight.

Boil the potatoes in salted water for 5 minutes, leave to cool, then cut into small chunks. Fry the potatoes in a little butter and oil until golden brown, adding the garlic for the last minute, then set aside to cool.

Grease a baking tray. Divide the dough into two equal pieces and flatten each into an oval shape about 24cm/9½ inches long. Place on the baking tray and leave to rise for 1–2 hours.

Preheat the oven to 230°C/450°F/gas mark 8. Sprinkle the dough lightly with flour. Cover the two pieces of dough equally with the potato mixture, pressing it in firmly. Sprinkle the dill over the top and bake for 25 minutes until golden brown. Transfer to a wire rack to cool.

CEREAL RYE

A German-based rye bread, full of seeds. If this was a wine it would be a full-bodied red.

350g (12oz) dark rye flour
150g (5½oz) strong white flour, plus extra for dusting
10g (⅓oz) salt
20g (¾oz) yeast
75ml (2½fl oz) malt extract
340ml (11½fl oz) water
2 teaspoons caraway seeds
75g (3oz) sunflower seeds
75g (3oz) sesame seeds
1 tablespoon poppy seeds

MAKES 2 LOAVES

Put all the ingredients into a bowl and mix well. Knead gently for 5 minutes to bring together, then tip out onto a lightly floured surface and knead with your fingers and palms for 6 minutes. Put the dough back in the bowl and leave to rest for 2 hours.

Grease two 450g (1lb) loaf tins. Divide the dough into two equal pieces and form each into a sausage shape. Put into the tins and leave to rise for 1 hour.

Preheat the oven to 220°C/425°F/gas mark 7. Bake for 30–35 minutes, then turn out onto a wire rack to cool.

SESAME RINGS

These breads have been spotted in bakeries around the Middle East, Greece and in the tombs of the Pharoahs. The rings can be cut open and filled with cheese and onion to make a great snack.

500g (1lb 2oz) strong white flour, plus extra for dusting
10g (⅓oz) salt
20g (¾oz) yeast
30ml (1fl oz) olive oil
300ml (½ pint) water
1 egg, beaten, for eggwash
Sesame seeds, to coat

MAKES 12 RINGS

Put all the ingredients, except the sesame seeds, into a bowl and roughly mix together. When the dough has formed, tip it onto a lightly floured surface and knead for 5 minutes. Put the dough back in the bowl and leave to double in size.

Line two baking trays. Divide the dough into 12 pieces and shape into sausages 25cm/10 inches long, then join the ends to form a ring. Space slightly apart on the baking trays. When all the rings have been made, brush with the eggwash, then sprinkle generously with sesame seeds. Place on the baking trays and leave to rise for 1 hour.

Preheat the oven to 220°C/425°F/gas mark 7. Bake for about 15 minutes until golden brown, then transfer to a wire rack to cool.

SUNFLOWER SEED BREAD

I was asked to make a bread for Spyros, a friend in Cyprus; he loved sunflower seeds so I came up with this. I hope you like it. It will last longer if the butter is omitted, but it gives it a richer flavour.

ILLUSTRATED

250g (9oz) wholemeal flour
250g (9oz) strong white flour,
  plus extra for dusting
10g (⅓oz) salt
20g (¾oz) yeast
50g (1¾oz) butter (optional)
150g (5½oz) sunflower seeds
300ml (½ pint) water

MAKES 1 LOAF

Put the flours, salt, yeast, butter (if using), 125g (4½oz) of the sunflower seeds and water into a large bowl and mix to a soft pliable dough (add a little extra water if necessary). Tip out onto a lightly floured surface and knead for 5–6 minutes until you have a very smooth dough, then put the dough back in the bowl and leave to rest for 1 hour.

Line a baking tray. Shape the dough into a ball and flatten with your hands to a 3cm/1¼ inch thickness. Using a knife, make vertical slashes around the edges of the dough, from top to bottom. Put onto the baking tray, then scatter the dough with the remaining sunflower seeds. Dust with flour and leave to rise in a warm place for 1 hour.

Preheat the oven to 220°C/425°F/gas mark 7. Bake for 30 minutes until golden brown, then transfer to a wire rack to cool.

RYE WITH CARAWAY

You'll either love or hate this loaf, mainly because of the caraway seeds. You need to start this the night before.

300g (10½oz) rye flour, plus extra for dusting
200g (7oz) strong white flour,
  plus extra for dusting
20g (¾oz) yeast
325ml (11fl oz) water
5g (⅛oz) salt
60g (2¼oz) butter, softened
1 tablespoon caraway seeds

MAKES 1 LOAF

Put half the rye flour, half the white flour and all the yeast into a large bowl, then add about 225ml (8fl oz) of water and mix well until you have a thick paste. Leave this dough in the bowl overnight for 10–12 hours.

Add the rest of the flours, the salt, butter, caraway seeds and remaining water and mix well in the bowl for 3 minutes. Tip out onto a lightly floured surface and knead well for 3 minutes, then put the dough back in the bowl and leave to rise for 1 hour.

Line a baking tray. Tip the dough out onto a floured surface and shape into a ball, then, using a rolling pin, flatten it slightly into a disc 3.5cm/1½ inches thick. Cover the top with rye flour, put the dough on the baking tray and leave to rise for 2 hours.

Preheat the oven to 220°C/425°F/gas mark 7. Bake for 30 minutes, then serve warm with smoked salmon.

FRUIT & NUT BREADS

STILTON & WALNUT WHOLEMEAL LOAF

This bread was one of the first breads I made when I worked at the Chester Grosvenor Hotel. It was produced for the restaurant and went well with the cheeseboard. It's a real old favourite. You can also make this bread with 100 per cent white flour. This will give a slightly different texture.

100g (3½oz) strong white flour, plus extra for dusting
400g (14oz) wholemeal flour
10g (⅓oz) salt
20g (¾oz) yeast
50g (1¾oz) butter, softened
300ml (½ pint) water
100g (3½oz) Stilton cheese, crumbled
125g (4½oz) walnuts, chopped

MAKES I LOAF

Put the flours, salt, yeast and butter into a bowl. Add the water, a little at a time, and gradually incorporate all the flour from the sides of the bowl.

Turn the dough out onto a lightly floured surface and knead for 5 minutes until it is smooth and pliable. Put the dough back in the bowl and leave to rise for 1 hour.

Line a baking tray. Add the Stilton and walnuts to the dough and mix well together. Divide the dough into three equal pieces and roll each one into a long sausage. Plait the dough – place the three strips side by side and join them at the top, then bring the right strip over the middle strip, then the left strip over, and continue until the plait is complete. Put on the tray and leave to rise for 1 hour.

Preheat the oven to 230°C/450°F/gas mark 8. Bake for 30–40 minutes, then transfer to a wire rack to cool.

FRUIT BREAD

Made on Good Friday, this bread is eaten throughout the Easter weekend, so you can throw the chocolates away.

600g (1lb 5oz) strong white flour,
   plus extra for dusting
5g (⅛oz) salt
20g (¾oz) yeast
75g (3oz) caster sugar
75g (3oz) butter, softened
2 medium eggs, beaten
275ml (9½fl oz) milk and water mixed
2 teaspoons ground cinnamon
50g (1¾oz) mandarin segments
75g (3oz) sultanas
60g (2¼oz) mixed peel
Zest of 3 lemons
Zest of 3 oranges

MAKES 2 LOAVES

Put the flour, salt, yeast, sugar, butter and eggs into a large bowl. Gradually add the milk and water mixture and bind the ingredients together for 3 minutes. Tip the dough out onto a lightly floured surface and knead for 5 minutes, then put the dough back in the bowl and leave for 1½ hours to rise.

Line a baking tray. Incorporate the remaining ingredients into the dough on a floured surface. Divide the dough into two equal pieces and shape each into balls. Place on the baking tray. Flatten the balls slightly. Using a floured knife, score each piece into eight equal segments, cutting right through to the tray. Leave to rise for 1 hour.

Preheat the oven to 220°C/425°F/gas mark 7. Bake for 20 minutes until golden brown, then transfer to a wire rack to cool.

DATE & FIG BREAD

This is a moist, chewy bread packed with goodness. For me it's a breakfast bread, but it would be equally at home on a cheeseboard. ILLUSTRATED

400g (14oz) wholemeal flour
100g (3½oz) strong white flour,
   plus extra for dusting
5g (⅛oz) salt
20g (¾oz) yeast
50g (1¾oz) butter, softened
1 tablespoon treacle
300ml (½ pint) water
75g (3oz) dried figs, chopped
75g (3oz) dates, chopped

MAKES 2 LOAVES

Put the flours, salt, yeast, butter, treacle and water into a bowl and mix for 5 minutes. Tip out onto a lightly floured surface and knead for 5 minutes, then put the dough back in the bowl and leave for 1 hour to rise.

Line a baking tray. Incorporate the figs and dates into the dough, then divide it into two equal pieces. Shape into balls, place on the baking tray and leave to rise for 1 hour.

Preheat the oven to 220°C/425°F/gas mark 7. Dust the loaves with flour and, using a knife, make three equidistant horizontal cuts all around each ball. Bake for 25 minutes, then transfer to a wire rack to cool.

GRAPE & SULTANA BREAD

This bread was inspired by a friend of mine, Chris Davies, an avid cook who wanted an unusual bread for his dinner guests. I think it did the trick!

500g (1lb 2oz) strong white flour,
   plus extra for dusting
5g (⅛oz) salt
30g (1oz) caster sugar
20g (¾oz) yeast
30g (1oz) butter, softened
300ml (½ pint) water
75g (3oz) red seedless grapes
75g (3oz) sultanas

MAKES 1 LOAF

Put the flour, salt, sugar, yeast and butter into a large bowl and mix together, then slowly add the water until all the flour has been incorporated (you might not need all of it). Tip out onto a lightly floured surface and, using your fingers and palms, knead for 5 minutes. Put the bread back in the bowl and leave to rest for 1 hour.

Line a baking tray. Add the grapes and sultanas to the dough and mix in well, then shape into a ball and flatten slightly using your hand. Put on the baking tray, dust the top with flour and leave to rise for 1 hour.

Preheat the oven to 200°C/400°F/gas mark 6. Score a square in the top of the dough and bake for 25–30 minutes. Transfer to a wire rack to cool.

DATE, PRUNE & PECAN BREAD

John Wood, the Executive Chef at Cliveden House, asked me to make a bread to complement his new cheeseboard, so after various experiments I came up with this one. Its sweet, slightly nutty flavour is delicious with Stilton and the stronger French cheeses – try it as a starter topped with baked Camembert and cranberries. ILLUSTRATED

15g (½oz) yeast
325ml (11fl oz) warm water
500g (1lb 2oz) wholemeal flour,
   plus extra for dusting
5g (⅛oz) salt
125g (4½oz) pecans, chopped
50g (1¾oz) butter, softened
150g (5½oz) dates, chopped
40g (1½oz) soft, ready-to-eat dried prunes,
   chopped

MAKES 2 LOAVES

Dilute the yeast in the water. Put the flour, salt and butter into a bowl and mix well with the yeasty water. Tip out onto a lightly floured surface and knead the dough for 5 minutes. Put the dough back in the bowl and leave to rest for 2 hours.

Divide the dough into two equal pieces and incorporate the pecans, dates and prunes into each piece, pressing in firmly. Knead for a further 5 minutes, then rest the dough for 1 hour. Line a baking tray.

Preheat the oven to 200°C/400°F/gas mark 6. Shape the pieces into two ovals and place on the baking tray. Dust with flour and, using a knife, cut a zigzag pattern on the top, then leave to rise for 1 hour. Bake for 35–40 minutes, then turn out onto a wire rack to cool.

WALNUT BREAD

This bread is a must on any cheeseboard. I would suggest serving it with a ripe Stilton or, failing that, try it with the creamy Savoyard cheese Reblochon – oh, and a glass of red wine.

350g (12oz) wholemeal flour
150g (5½oz) strong white flour,
  plus extra for dusting
10g (⅓oz) salt
20g (¾oz) yeast
40g (1½oz) butter, softened
60ml (2fl oz) walnut oil
250ml (9fl oz) water
150g (5½oz) walnut pieces

MAKES 1 LOAF

Put all the ingredients into a large bowl, then mix well with your hands for 4 minutes. When all the flour has been incorporated, tip the dough out onto a lightly floured surface and, using your fingers and the heel of your palm, knead for 5 minutes. Put the dough back in the bowl and leave to rise for 1 hour.

Line a baking tray. Shape the dough into a ball and dust with white flour. Place on the baking tray and leave to rise for 1 hour.

Preheat the oven to 220°C/425°F/gas mark 7. Using a sharp knife, cut a cross into the top of the dough, then bake for 30 minutes until golden. Transfer to a wire rack to cool.

WALNUT & SULTANA BREAD

This bread was originally made while I was head baker at The Dorchester Hotel in London. It was baked for the breakfast menu, but quickly made its way to the cheese trolley – it's great with most cheeses.

400g (14oz) wholemeal flour
100g (3½oz) strong white flour,
  plus extra for dusting
10g (⅓oz) salt
20g (¾oz) yeast
60g (2¼oz) butter, softened
350ml (12fl oz) water
125g (4½oz) walnut pieces
100g (3½oz) sultanas

MAKES 1 LOAF

Put all the ingredients, except the water, walnuts and sultanas, into a bowl, then slowly add the water and, using your hands, bind the ingredients together. When all the flour has been incorporated, tip the dough out onto a lightly floured surface and, using your fingers and the heel of your palm, knead for 5 minutes. Put the dough back in the bowl and leave to rise for 2 hours.

Line a baking tray. Incorporate the walnuts and sultanas into the dough, shape into a ball and make a hole in the middle with your finger. Slowly begin to open the hole until it is about 5cm/2 inches across. Place on the baking tray, dust with white flour and leave to rise for 1 hour.

Preheat the oven to 230°C/450°F/gas mark 8. Bake for 30 minutes until golden, then transfer to a wire rack to cool. Serve with cheese, or at breakfast, toasted with butter.

APRICOT RYE

This is a very German way of making rye bread and the apricot adds a lovely fruity kick to an already fantastic loaf. You need to start this the day before.

300g (10½oz) rye flour, plus extra for dusting
200g (7oz) strong white flour, plus extra for dusting
20g (¾oz) yeast
350ml (12fl oz) water
10g (⅓oz) salt
60g (2¼oz) butter, softened
125g (4½oz) dried apricots, chopped

MAKES 1 LOAF

Put half the rye flour, half the white flour and all the yeast into a bowl. Then add about 200ml (7fl oz) of water and mix well until you have a thick paste. Leave this overnight for 10–12 hours.

Add the rest of the flours and water, the salt, butter and apricots to the dough and mix well for 3 minutes, then tip out onto a lightly floured surface and knead well for 3 minutes. Put the dough back in the bowl and leave to rise for 1 hour.

Line a baking tray. Shape the dough into a sausage and taper the ends. Place on the baking tray and leave to rise for 1 hour.

Preheat the oven to 230°C/450°F/gas mark 8. Rub rye flour all over the top of the dough and, using a knife, cut zigzags down the centre of the loaf. Bake for 30 minutes, then transfer to a wire rack to cool.

CHOCOLATE & SOUR CHERRY BREAD

An incredibly luxurious bread that will be eaten in one sitting. If there is any left, use it to make extra-rich bread and butter pudding. This is definitely not a bread to count calories with!

500g (1lb 2oz) strong white flour, plus extra for dusting
1 teaspoon salt
30ml (1fl oz) olive oil
15g (½oz) yeast
300ml (½ pint) warm water
160g (5¾oz) can black cherries, drained
200g (7oz) chocolate chips

MAKES 2 LOAVES

Put the flour into a bowl with the salt, olive oil and yeast. Slowly add the warm water and mix by hand until the dough is pliable.

Tip the dough out onto a lightly floured surface and knead for 4–7 minutes. Put the dough back in the bowl and leave to rest for 1 hour.

Line a baking tray. Pat the cherries dry on kitchen paper. Work the chocolate chips and then the cherries into the dough. If the dough becomes too elastic to work in the cherries, leave to stand for 10 minutes, then try again. (You may need to add a little more flour if the mix becomes too sloppy.) Cut the dough in half, then shape into two balls and flatten to about 5cm/2 inches high. Place on the baking tray, dust heavily with flour and score diagonal lines across the top to form diamond shapes. Leave the dough to rest for 1 hour.

Preheat the oven to 200°C/400°F/gas mark 6. Bake for 20–25 minutes, then transfer to a wire rack to cool.

Fruit & Nut Breads

BANANA & MUESLI BREAD

This is comfort food at its best – rich and filling. Eat it toasted for tea, dripping with butter or, better still, piled high with baked apples or peaches with a dollop of fresh vanilla ice cream on top.

500g (1lb 2oz) wholemeal flour
10g (⅓oz) salt
15g (½oz) yeast
50g (1¾oz) butter, softened
320ml (11fl oz) water
100g (3½oz) muesli
2 large bananas, chopped

MAKES 2 LOAVES

Put the flour, salt, yeast and butter into a bowl. Slowly add water to the bowl and mix carefully by hand until the dough becomes elastic. Knead the dough for 5 minutes, then cover the bowl and set aside to rest for 2 hours.

Scatter the muesli onto the surface and tip the dough out onto it, using your hands to 'mash' the banana into the mixture. The dough will now be sticky, so add enough muesli to regain the original texture. Divide the dough in half.

Line a baking tray. Roll each piece of dough into a ball, then press into the remaining muesli, so that the dough becomes completely coated. Place the balls on the baking tray, flatten out slightly and leave to rise for 1–2 hours.

Preheat the oven to 200°C/400°F/gas mark 6. Using a knife, deeply score the top of each ball into eight sections. Bake for 25–30 minutes, then transfer to a wire rack to cool.

LEMON & ORANGE BREAD

I was inspired to make this bread when I visited a small artisan bakery in Tours, France. The baker produced a bread with oranges, saffron and honey made from a traditional recipe favoured by famous local poet François Rabelais. My twist was to try it with oranges and lemons – I think it works well.

400g (14oz) strong white flour,
  plus extra for dusting
125g (4½oz) rye flour
10g (⅓oz) salt
60g (2¼oz) butter, softened
60g (2¼oz) caster sugar
20g (¾oz) yeast
Zest of 5 lemons
Zest of 6 oranges
300ml (½ pint) water

MAKES I LOAF

Put all the ingredients into a bowl and massage together with your hands for 3 minutes. Tip the dough out onto a lightly floured surface and knead for 5 minutes. (The dough will discolour slightly, but don't worry.) Put the dough back in the bowl and leave to rise for 1 hour.

Line a baking tray. Shape the dough into a ball and push your finger down through the middle until you can feel the surface underneath. Using a sharp knife, cut across the top several times, then place on the baking tray and leave to rise for 1 hour.

Preheat the oven to 220°C/425°F/gas mark 7. Bake for 30 minutes until golden brown, then transfer to a wire rack to cool.

ORANGE, LEMON & CHERRY BREAD

Toasted with butter – perfect.

500g (1lb 2oz) strong white flour,
  plus extra for dusting
10g (⅓oz) salt
30g (1oz) caster sugar
40g (1½oz) butter, softened
20g (¾oz) yeast
Zest of 1 lemon
Zest of 3 oranges
300ml (½ pint) water
75g (3oz) morello cherries, pitted and halved

MAKES I LOAF

Put all the ingredients, except the cherries, into a bowl and mix to form a dough. Tip the dough out onto a lightly floured surface and knead for 5 minutes, then put back into the bowl and leave to rest for 1 hour.

Line a baking tray. Working on a well-floured surface, add the cherries to the dough and mix well, then divide the dough into two equal pieces and shape each into a sausage 40cm/16 inches long. Twist the two pieces together and place on the baking tray, then leave to rise for 1 hour.

Preheat the oven to 200°C/400°F/gas mark 6. Bake for 25 minutes, then transfer to a wire rack to cool.

HONEY & SAFFRON LOAF

The subtle flavours and smells in this bread are unique. Saffron works well with dough, but you could also try mango chutney – just replace the saffron with 75g (3oz) of chutney: yummy!

250g (9oz) strong white flour
250g (9oz) wholemeal flour
20g (¾oz) yeast
275ml (9½fl oz) water
10g (⅓oz) salt
75ml (2½fl oz) honey
1 teaspoon saffron strands diluted in 1 tablespoon water

MAKES 1 LOAF

Put half the white flour, half the wholemeal flour and all the yeast into a bowl and add 200ml (7fl oz) of water. Whisk together for 5 minutes, then leave for 4 hours.

Add the remaining flours and water, the salt, honey and saffron to the dough, and knead well for 5 minutes. Leave in the bowl to rest for 30 minutes.

Line a baking tray. Shape the dough into a ball, place on the tray and leave to rise for 1 hour.

Preheat the oven to 220°C/425°F/gas mark 7. Score around the middle of the loaf with a knife and bake for 30 minutes. Transfer to a wire rack to cool.

PEANUT BREAD

This bread is always a great favourite with the kids at teatime, loaded with honey or chocolate spread. For a change, serve it with cream cheese and celery as an energy-giving sandwich.

500g (1lb 2oz) strong white flour, plus extra for dusting
1 teaspoon salt
300g (10½oz) crunchy peanut butter
15g (½oz) yeast
350ml (12fl oz) warm water
100g (3½oz) caramelized peanut chips

MAKES 2 LOAVES

Put the flour, salt, peanut butter and yeast into a bowl. Slowly add the warm water and mix by hand until the dough is pliable. Leave in the bowl to rest for 1 hour. Work in the peanut chips, then leave to rest again for 1 hour.

Grease a baking tray. Punch any air out of the dough and divide it into two equal pieces. Mould into two sausage shapes 50cm/20 inches long and each thick at one end and tapering to a point at the other. Starting from the thick ends, roll them up into loose coils, place on the baking tray and leave to prove for 1 hour.

Preheat the oven to 200°C/400°F/gas mark 6. Dust each loaf lightly with flour. Bake for 25 minutes, then transfer to a wire rack to cool.

ALMOND BREAD

A bread I devised while I was in Cyprus; it's gorgeous toasted and with lashings of butter.

500g (1lb 2oz) strong white flour
5g (⅛oz) salt
60g (2¼oz) caster sugar
40g (1½oz) butter, softened
75g (3oz) ground almonds
20g (¾oz) yeast
300ml (½ pint) milk and water mixed
125g (4½oz) flaked almonds

MAKES 1 LOAF

Put the flour, salt, sugar, butter, ground almonds and yeast into a bowl. Add the milk and water mix and blend for 2 minutes. Tip the dough out onto a lightly floured surface and knead with your hands until it becomes soft and pliable. This should take no more than 5 minutes. Put the dough back in the bowl and leave to rise for 1 hour.

Line a baking tray. Tip the dough out onto a floured surface and mix in half the flaked almonds. Flatten the dough into an oval shape about 3cm/1¼ inches thick and place on the baking tray. Top the dough with the remaining flaked almonds, pressing them down firmly. Leave to rise for 1 hour.

Preheat the oven to 220°C/425°F/gas mark 7. Bake for 25–30 minutes, then transfer to a wire rack to cool.

APPLE & SULTANA DANISH PASTRIES

My wife's favourite Danish. Remember Valentine's Day – get baking. You probably won't use all the pastries at once, so you can freeze the finished dough for up to three months. You need to start this the day before.

FOR THE PASTRY
20g (¾oz) yeast
375ml (13fl oz) warm water
625g (1lb 6oz) strong white flour,
   plus extra for dusting
5g (⅛oz) salt
75g (3oz) caster sugar
500g (1lb 2oz) butter, chilled

FOR THE FILLING
6 tart dessert apples, peeled, cored
   and sliced
100g (3½oz) sultanas
1 teaspoon ground cinnamon
1 egg, beaten, for eggwash
Apricot jam, warmed, to glaze

FOR THE WATER ICING
150g (5½oz) icing sugar
Water

MAKES 18 DANISH PASTRIES

Dilute the yeast in the water and put with the flour, salt and sugar into a large mixing bowl. Using a wooden spoon, mix until the dough becomes pliable. Tip the dough out onto a lightly floured surface and knead well until it feels elastic. Put the dough back in the bowl and refrigerate for 1 hour.

Return the chilled dough to a floured work surface and roll it into a 60 x 30.5cm/ 24 x 12 inch rectangle. Put the butter between two sheets of clingfilm and flatten with a rolling pin to a 40 x 30cm/16 x 12 inch rectangle. Peel away the clingfilm and lay the butter over one end of the dough. Bring the uncovered third of the

dough into the centre, then fold the covered third over, so that your dough is now in three layers. Return the dough to the fridge to chill for 1 hour.

Scatter some more flour over the work surface and roll out the dough to the same size rectangle as before. Repeat the folding process, one side on top of the other, and place the dough back in the fridge for 1 hour. You will need to repeat this process twice more before leaving the dough to rest, wrapped in clingfilm, overnight.

Line two baking trays. Cut the dough in half and roll out each piece to a 37cm/15 inch square. Cut into nine 12.5cm/5 inch squares. Fold the edges into the middle so you have a parcel, place on the baking trays and leave to rise for 2 hours at an ambient temperature (20°C+/68°F+).

Meanwhile, cook the apples in a pan with a little water to soften them for 7 minutes, then add the sultanas and cinnamon and allow to cool.

Spoon the apple mixture into the middle of each dough square. Preheat the oven to 200°C/400°F/ gas mark 6. Brush the eggwash onto the exposed parts of the dough and bake for 15–20 minutes. Remove from the oven and brush with warmed apricot jam.

While the pastries are cooling, make a water icing. Tip the icing sugar into a bowl, add a little water (1½ tablespoons) and mix in well, then gradually add more water until the icing coats the back of a spoon. Top the pastries with the icing and serve.

STRAWBERRY DANISH PASTRIES

Once you've prepared the dough and cut out the shapes you can freeze them for use later, if you wish.

1 quantity Danish Pastry dough (*see* page 121)

FOR THE FILLING
200g (7oz) strawberries, quartered
125ml (4fl oz) extra-thick strawberry yogurt
200ml (7fl oz) custard
2 tablespoons caster sugar
1 egg, beaten, for eggwash
5 tablespoons flaked almonds
Apricot jam, warmed, to glaze

MAKES 18 DANISH PASTRIES

Make the pastry as on page 121, up to the point where it is chilled overnight.

Line two baking trays. Cut the dough in half and roll out each piece to a 38cm/15 inch square. Cut into nine 12.5cm/5 inch squares.

Add the strawberries to the yogurt and fold in the custard. Spoon the mixture down the middle of each of the squares and fold in half lengthways. Pinch the dough together around the edge. Using a knife, score the tops of the dough. Brush with the eggwash and sprinkle the flaked almonds all over the tops. Put the dough on the baking trays and leave to rise for 1 hour.

Preheat the oven to 200°C/400°F/gas mark 6. Bake for 15–20 minutes until golden brown. Transfer to a wire rack to cool.

Put some apricot jam in a small saucepan with a splash of water and bring to the boil. Brush this onto the Danish pastries and serve.

PAIN AU RAISIN DANISH PASTRIES

This was a favourite of mine at Cliveden House in the morning, eaten with a cup of tea, while sitting by the window looking at the view across the grounds.
ILLUSTRATED

1 quantity Danish Pastry dough (*see* page 121)

FOR THE FILLING
200ml (7fl oz) fresh custard
250g (9oz) raisins or sultanas
1 teaspoon ground cinnamon
1 egg, beaten, for eggwash
Apricot jam, warmed, to glaze

½ quantity Water Icing (*see* page 121)

MAKES ABOUT 20 DANISH PASTRIES

Make the pastry as on page 121, up to the point where it is chilled overnight.

Line two baking trays. Cut the dough in half and roll out each piece to a 38 x 30cm/ 15 x 12 inch rectangle. Spread the custard over the top and sprinkle liberally with the raisins or sultanas, sprinkle with the cinnamon and roll each up along the long side into a sausage. Cut into 3cm/1¼ inch pieces, place flat-side down on the baking trays and leave to rise for 1½ hours.

Preheat the oven to 200°C/400°F/gas mark 6. Brush the pastries lightly with the eggwash and bake for 15–20 minutes until golden brown. Transfer to a wire rack and brush with warm apricot jam. Leave to cool, then top with the water icing.

SALLY LUNN

This bread reminds me of a little bakery near to where I was brought up in Merseyside. On my way back from school I would buy a Sally Lunn and eat it with butter when I got home.

400g (14oz) strong white flour, plus extra for dusting
10g (⅓oz) salt
40g (1½oz) caster sugar
40g (1½oz) butter, softened
20g (¾oz) yeast
120ml (4fl oz) milk
120ml (4fl oz) water
50g (1¾oz) sultanas
60g (2¼oz) glacé cherries, halved
1 teaspoon ground cinnamon
Zest of 3 oranges

½ quantity Water Icing (*see* page 121)

MAKES I LOAF

Put the flour, salt, sugar, butter, yeast, milk and water into a bowl and mix together with your hands. When all the flour has been incorporated, tip the dough out onto a lightly floured surface and knead until smooth and pliable. Put the dough back in the bowl and leave to rest for 1 hour.

Line a baking tray. Add the sultanas, cherries, cinnamon and orange zest to the dough and, using an electric mixer (with the blade attachment) or your hands, work it in well. Shape the dough into a sausage shape about 23cm/9 inches long. Place the dough on the baking tray and leave to rise for 1 hour.

Preheat the oven to 200°C/400°F/gas mark 6. Bake for 25 minutes, then transfer to a wire rack to cool. Drizzle the water icing over the top of the bread. Cut into slices and eat with lashings of butter.

TEACAKES

These are great toasted, with butter.

400g (14oz) strong white flour, plus extra for dusting
5g (⅛oz) salt
40g (1½oz) caster sugar
1 teaspoon ground cinnamon
50g (1¾oz) butter, softened
20g (¾oz) yeast
240ml (8½fl oz) water
75g (3oz) sultanas
60g (2¼oz) mixed peel
1 egg, beaten, for eggwash

MAKES 12 TEACAKES

Put the flour, salt, sugar, cinnamon, butter, yeast and water into a large bowl and mix together for 2 minutes. Tip the dough out onto a lightly floured surface and knead for 5 minutes, then put back in the bowl and leave to rest for 1 hour.

Line a large baking tray. Add the sultanas and mixed peel to the dough and divide into 12 pieces. Shape each piece into a ball and place on the baking tray. Flatten slightly with the palm of your hand and leave to rise for 1 hour.

Preheat the oven to 190°C/375°F/gas mark 5. Brush the teacakes with the eggwash and bake for 15 minutes.

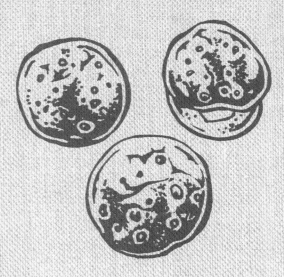

HOLLYWOOD HOT CROSS BUNS

I wanted to go back to the way we used to make hot cross buns, using fresh fruit rather than all dried. The result are these juicy buns – the kids will love them, and so will the adults!

500g (1lb 2oz) strong white flour, plus extra for dusting

5g (⅛oz) salt

75g (3oz) caster sugar

2 teaspoons ground cinnamon

30g (1oz) yeast

300ml (½ pint) milk and water mixed

60g (2¼oz) mandarin segments, chopped

60g (2¼oz) peaches, chopped

60g (2¼oz) apples, chopped

60g (2¼oz) apricot jam, warmed, to glaze

1 egg, beaten, for eggwash

FOR THE CROSSES

100ml (3½fl oz) water

125g (4½oz) flour

1 medium egg

MAKES 12 HOT CROSS BUNS

Put the flour, salt, sugar, cinnamon and yeast into a bowl. Slowly add enough of the milk and water mix to achieve a pliable dough. Tip out onto a lightly floured surface and knead well for 5 minutes, then put the dough back in the bowl and leave to rise for 1 hour.

Working on a floured surface, incorporate the mandarins, peaches and apples into the dough.

Line a baking tray. Divide the dough into twelve 75g (3oz) pieces and roll each into a ball. Put them on the baking tray and leave to rest for 1 hour.

Preheat the oven to 200°C/400°F/gas mark 6. To make the crosses, whisk together the water, flour and egg to a smooth paste. Transfer to a polythene bag, squeeze into one corner and snip off the tip. Brush the buns with eggwash and, using the flour mixture, pipe a cross on top of each bun. Bake for 20 minutes until golden brown. Remove from the oven and brush them with warmed apricot jam. Serve immediately.

DOUGHNUTS

An obvious treat for my son Joshua, and a favourite of mine when I'm watching a film on those cold winter days.

250g (9oz) strong white flour, plus extra for dusting
Pinch of salt
40g (1½oz) caster sugar
30g (1oz) butter, softened
150ml (¼ pint) water
20g (¾oz) yeast
Vegetable or sunflower oil, for frying
Caster sugar, to coat

MAKES 6 DOUGHNUTS

Put all the ingredients, except the oil and coating sugar, into a large bowl and mix together, then tip out onto a lightly floured surface and knead for 5 minutes. Put the dough back in the bowl and leave to double in size.

Divide the dough into six equal pieces and shape into balls. Put on the floured surface and leave to rise until doubled in size.

Pour some oil into a large heavy-based pan and heat to 170°C/340°F, or a medium heat. Lower each of the doughnuts into the oil and fry until brown, then roll them over and fry the other side. (If you have a problem rolling the doughnuts over, then pierce them slightly with a knife.) The frying should take no more than 5 minutes in total. When they are browned, tip them into a bowl full of caster sugar and coat well. Cool on a wire rack, then enjoy with a cup of tea.

SWEET
TREATS

BROWN BREAD ICE CREAM

This has to be the easiest ice cream to make and it is absolutely delicious. Serve it stuffed into baked pears or peaches or as a sweet pancake filling – unbelievable!

75g (3oz) brown breadcrumbs, made from
  Guinness & Treacle Bread (*see* page 28)
60g (2¼oz) brown sugar
3 large eggs, separated
1 tablespoon dark rum
270ml (9½fl oz) double cream
75g (3oz) icing sugar

SERVES 4–6

Mix the breadcrumbs and sugar together, then spread in a thin layer on a baking tray and grill for 8 minutes or until dark and caramelized. When the mixture is cool, break up into small, bite-sized pieces.

Whisk the egg whites until stiff. In a separate bowl, mix the egg yolks with the rum, then fold this mixture into the egg whites. Finally, whisk the cream and icing sugar together until softly peaking, then, using a metal spoon, fold the cream and breadcrumbs into the egg mixture. Pour into a metal container and freeze for about 4 hours before serving.

CROISSANT PUDDING

This has the edge over traditional bread and butter pudding – the buttery croissants and tartness of the blueberries really lift this dish.

5 croissants (*see* page 48)
75g (3oz) blackberries, plus a few extra to serve
75g (3oz) blueberries, plus a few extra to serve
75g (3oz) raspberries, plus a few extra to serve
Splash of Kirsch
Icing sugar

FOR THE SAUCE ANGLAISE
500ml (18fl oz) milk
1 vanilla pod, split lengthways
4 medium eggs
50g (1¾oz) caster sugar

SERVES 6

Preheat the oven to 180°C/350°F/gas mark 4. Cut the croissants lengthways and place in a shallow ovenproof dish. Sprinkle over the berries and add a splash of Kirsch.

To make the sauce anglaise, put the milk and vanilla pod in a pan and bring to the boil. In a bowl, whisk the eggs and sugar together to a froth, then pour the milk onto the eggs, whisking well. Lift out the vanilla pod and scrape out the seeds. Return the seeds to the bowl and whisk to combine. Pour over the croissants and leave to stand for 15 minutes.

Bake for 25 minutes. Remove from the oven, sprinkle generously with the icing sugar and caramelize with a blow torch or under the grill. Serve with pouring cream and more berries.

SAVARIN WITH CHOCOLATE SAUCE & EGGS

I made this recipe for Easter some years back. It appeals to both children and adults alike.

FOR THE SAVARIN
450g (1lb) strong white flour
175ml (6fl oz) milk
50g (1¾oz) yeast
Pinch of salt
60g (2¼oz) caster sugar
4 medium eggs
200g (7oz) butter, very soft

FOR THE CHOCOLATE SAUCE
200g (7oz) milk chocolate, melted
300ml (½ pint) vanilla custard

TO DECORATE
Apricot jam, warmed
Mini chocolate eggs

SERVES 8

To make the savarin, put all the ingredients into a bowl and mix together. Beat well for 6 minutes until smooth, then place in a greased and floured savarin ring and leave to rise for 1 hour until light to the touch.

Preheat the oven to 200°C/400°F/gas mark 6. Bake for 25 minutes until golden brown.

Meanwhile, make the chocolate sauce by stirring the melted chocolate into the custard.

Tip the savarin out of the ring and brush with warm apricot jam. Fill the centre with the chocolate sauce and top with mini chocolate eggs.

BLUEBERRY MUFFINS

These muffins are great eaten warm and covered with pouring cream, or serve them cold as a snack. Either way, they're a winner. ILLUSTRATED

250g (9oz) butter, softened
185g (6½oz) caster sugar
4 medium eggs, beaten
250g (9oz) strong white flour
1½ teaspoons baking powder
200g (7oz) blueberries
Icing sugar, for dusting

MAKES 16 MUFFINS

Preheat the oven to 200°C/400°F/gas mark 6. In a bowl, cream the butter and sugar together until white and fluffy, then add the eggs, one at a time, beating well after each addition. Sift in the flour and baking powder, and mix to a smooth paste.

Line a muffin tray with paper cases and drop a spoonful of the mixture into each case. Scatter the blueberries over the top of each muffin.

Bake for 20–25 minutes or until the muffins spring back when pressed. Transfer to a wire rack to cool, then dust lightly with icing sugar.

WIMBLEDON MUFFINS

These muffins are just spectacular served at teatime with a dollop of clotted cream, preferably accompanying cucumber sandwiches and a cup of Earl Grey tea – anyone for tennis?

250g (9oz) butter, softened
185g (6½oz) caster sugar
5 medium eggs, beaten
250g (9oz) strong white flour
1½ teaspoons baking powder
16 medium-size strawberries,
    sliced into thirds
Icing sugar, for dusting

MAKES 16 MUFFINS

Preheat the oven to 200°C/400°F/gas mark 6. In a bowl, cream the butter and sugar together until white and fluffy, then add the eggs, one at a time, beating well after each addition. Sift in the flour and baking powder and mix to a smooth paste.

Line a muffin tray with paper cases and drop a spoonful of the mixture into each case. Gently press the sliced strawberries into the centre of each muffin.

Bake for 20–25 minutes or until the muffins spring back when pressed. Transfer to a wire rack to cool, then dust lightly with icing sugar.

PANCAKES WITH BANANAS & CREAM

I've included pancakes in this book mainly because they contain flour, and when I was working in hotels these recipes, along with some tarts and pies, were still under the jurisdiction of the baker rather than the pastry chef.

This recipe is very simple to make and the pancakes are delicious served on a bed of cream with raspberry sauce rippled through it.

FOR 10—12 PANCAKES
250g (9oz) white flour
30g (1oz) caster sugar
1 egg
450ml (16fl oz) milk
Sunflower oil, for frying

FOR THE FILLING (FILLS 4 PANCAKES)
20g (¾oz) butter
2 bananas, chopped
1 tablespoon dark rum
100ml (3½fl oz) whipped cream
150ml (¼ pint) fresh custard

Pouring cream (optional), to decorate
Raspberry sauce (optional), to decorate

SERVES 2

Whisk together the flour, 20g (¾oz) of the sugar, the egg and milk for 5 minutes. You should now have a batter mixture. Test it by dipping a spoon in the batter and seeing if it coats the back of the spoon evenly.

Heat a little sunflower oil in a frying pan and leave to smoke. Pour half a cup of batter in the middle of the pan, tilt the pan to move the batter to the edges and replace on the heat for 2 minutes. Turn the pancake over with a spatula and fry for another 2 minutes. Remove from the pan and put on a plate to cool. Repeat with the remaining batter. (The batter will make up to 12 pancakes. Any leftover pancakes can be kept in the freezer, interleaved with squares of parchment paper.)

To make the filling, melt the butter in the frying pan, add the bananas and cook for 1 minute. Add the rum and flambé until the flames die down, then set aside.

Whisk the cream with the remaining sugar until peaking and spoon a little into the middle of four of the pancakes. Top each with a little custard and the bananas, roll up and serve on a pool of pouring cream rippled with raspberry sauce, if so desired – watch those waistlines!

NORMANDY APPLE TART

My father and mother were both excellent at making pastry and I grew up knowing how to make good sweet pastry. Some pastry work is essential to becoming a good baker – it gives you a little edge on the competition. I had this tart in Chinon in the Loire Valley with a glass of Chablis for lunch, delicious! You'll only need half the pastry for this, so freeze the rest for another time.

FOR THE PASTRY

375g (13oz) strong white flour, plus extra for dusting

250g (9oz) caster sugar

125g (4½oz) butter, softened

2 medium eggs

1 tablespoon cold water

2 dessert apples, cored and thinly sliced

100g (3½oz) apricot jam, warmed

FOR THE FRANGIPANE

200g (7oz) butter, softened

200g (7oz) caster sugar

2 medium eggs

2 medium egg yolks

Splash of Calvados

60g (2¼oz) plain flour

200g (7oz) ground almonds

SERVES 8

Preheat the oven to 200°C/400°F/gas mark 6. To make the sweet pastry, put the flour, sugar, butter, eggs and water in a food processor and blend to a smooth paste. Wrap and chill for 1 hour. Roll out on a lightly floured surface and use to line a 25cm/ 10 inch loose-based tart tin.

To make the frangipane, cream the butter and sugar together and add the eggs and egg yolks one at a time. Add the Calvados, flour and ground almonds, and mix well. Spread the frangipane over the paste in the tin, then fan out the apple slices from the edge to the middle in the form of a cross.

Bake for 35–40 minutes until golden brown and just firm. Brush with the warm apricot jam while still warm and serve immediately.

HOLLYWOOD MINCE PIES

My twist on the traditional recipe. The addition of real fruit lifts the pies to new heights. Remember when lining the moulds to keep the pastry thin and add plenty of filling.

FOR THE PASTRY

375g (13oz) strong white flour
250g (9oz) butter, softened
125g (4½oz) caster sugar, plus extra for sprinkling
2 medium eggs
1 tablespoon cold water
1 egg, beaten, for eggwash
Icing sugar, for dusting

FOR THE FILLING

400g (14oz) mincemeat
125g (4½oz) can of mandarins (drained weight), drained and chopped
2 apples, finely diced

MAKES ABOUT 24 MINCE PIES

Preheat the oven to 200°C/400°F/gas mark 6. To make the sweet pastry, put the flour, butter, sugar, eggs and water in a food processor and blend to a smooth paste. Wrap and chill for 1 hour.

To make the filling, mix together the mincemeat, mandarins and apples in a bowl.

Use two 12-hole muffin or cupcake trays. Thinly roll out the pastry and cut out twenty-four 8cm/3¼ inch rounds to line the bottom and sides of the holes and fill with the mincemeat. Cut out 6cm/2½ inch rounds for lids. Brush the top edges of the bases with the eggwash and position the lids, pressing down gently around the edges to seal. Prick the lids with a knife and brush with the eggwash.

Bake for 20 minutes, then transfer to a wire rack to cool. Dust with icing sugar and serve warm with fresh cream.

APPLE PIE

A very French recipe my mother-in-law is famous for. The cinnamon really adds another dimension to this pie.

FOR THE PASTRY
375g (13oz) strong white flour
250g (9oz) caster sugar
125g (4½oz) butter, softened
3 medium eggs
100g (3½oz) ground almonds
1 tablespoon cold water

FOR THE FILLING
1.25kg (2¾lb) apples, peeled, cored
  and sliced
Splash of Calvados
4 tablespoons lemon juice
Handful of sultanas
Pinch of ground cinnamon
100g (3½oz) caster sugar

FOR THE TOPPING
1 egg, beaten, for eggwash
Caster sugar, for sprinkling

SERVES 8

Soak the sliced apples in the Calvados and lemon juice for 2 hours. To make the sweet pastry, put the flour, sugar, butter, eggs, ground almonds and water in a food processor and blend to a smooth paste. Wrap and chill for 1 hour.

Preheat the oven to 200°C/400°F/gas mark 6. Roll out the pastry to fit a 30.5cm/12 inch pie tin or foil base and fill with the soaked apples and sultanas. Sprinkle with the cinnamon. Roll out the pastry trimmings to make a lid, cover the pie and crimp the edges together. Brush with the eggwash, sprinkle with sugar and bake for about 40 minutes until golden brown.

Sweet Treats

APPLE & PEAR PIE WITH FRUIT SAUCE

I was first introduced to sweet pastry by my mother, Gill – she gave me this recipe and it's the best! The pastry will keep, wrapped in clingfilm, in the fridge for one week. ILLUSTRATED

FOR THE PASTRY
375g (13oz) strong white flour
250g (9oz) caster sugar
125g (4½oz) butter, softened
2 medium eggs
1 tablespoon cold water

FOR THE FILLING
4 dessert apples, peeled, cored and chopped
5 large pears, peeled, cored and chopped
40g (1½oz) sugar

FOR THE TOPPING
1 egg, beaten, for eggwash
Caster sugar, for sprinkling

FOR THE FRUIT SAUCE
300g (10½oz) raspberries
Icing sugar

SERVES 8

Preheat the oven to 200°C/400°F/gas mark 6. To make the pastry, put the flour, sugar, butter, eggs and water in a food processor and blend to a smooth paste. Wrap and chill for 1 hour.

To make the filling, put the fruit and sugar in a pan and cook over a medium heat for 5 minutes to soften the fruit. Set aside to cool.

Roll out the pastry to fit a 30.5cm/12 inch pie plate and spoon on the filling. Roll out the pastry trimmings to make a lid and place on top. Trim the pastry edges and crimp around the edge, brush with the eggwash and sprinkle with sugar. Bake for about 40 minutes until golden brown.

Meanwhile, make the raspberry sauce. Pass the raspberries through a sieve, then stir in a little icing sugar, to taste. Serve with the pie.

Page numbers in italics indicate illustrations